GW00643008

Where the Birds Sing

Wild Places for the Soul

Jane Upchurch

To Liz
with love from
Jane 12/12

Onwards and Upwards Publishers

Berkeley House, 11 Nightingale Crescent, Leatherhead, Surrey, KT24 6PD.
www.onwardsandupwards.org

Copyright © Jane Upchurch 2012

The right of Jane Upchurch to be identified as the author of this work has been asserted by the author in accordance with the Copyright, Designs and Patents Act 1988.

All rights reserved.

No part of this publication may be reproduced or transmitted in any form or by any means, electronic or mechanical, including photocopy, recording or any information storage and retrieval system, without permission in writing from the author or publisher.

Printed in the UK.

ISBN: 978-1-907509-62-9
Cover design: Guilherme Gustavo Condeixa

The opinions represented in this book are the author's own and do not necessarily reflect the position and views of the publisher, its employees and associates.

About the Author

Jane's writing links a love of this planet, its rocks and oceans, trees and bees, with awareness of the intimacy and wildness of God. It is a way of growing closer to the things she writes about; it is a way of growing in love.

Her journey has included living in community at the Findhorn Foundation, celebrating Jewish festivals with her family and hosting a church in her home. Her writing bridges Christian and holistic spirituality. She particularly likes the concept in Celtic spirituality of creation as a self-giving of God.

She has qualifications in biology, geology and theology as well as counselling, education and pastoral studies. She has worked with young people, the unemployed and people with a mental health or substance abuse problem. She home-schooled her daughters when they were young.

Jane is a spiritual companion; she takes services in a local church and runs groups in the community including a meditation group. She is a member of a dance company and loves Cole Porter, crime novels and colour. She lives on the Western edge of London with her husband Bill, her daughters Joy and Grace and her dog Jenny.

www.janeupchurch.co.uk

Contents

"There is another dimension; there is a spiritual and life-changing engagement with the wild world available out there to everyone, a private, personal wildness we can still relocate in our heads and which can serve us well by bringing us closer to the dazzling creative genius of the very nature that made us what we are." [1]

- John Lister-Kaye –

---

[1] From AT THE WATER'S EDGE
by John Lister-Kaye,
first published in Great Britain by
Canongate Books Ltd, 14 High Street, Edinburgh, EH1 1TE

Introduction

'Wild' has undergone a transformation. There was a time when the wild was a scary place beyond our borders and our influence, somewhere wolves or tigers reigned and could eat you for breakfast. The wild was a place to be avoided or domesticated. When applied to a person or event it was an insult; it is now a compliment.

In the developed world, we have filled our lands and our minds with our own activities. We have done our best to shut out the wild, and now we realize we need it. We need places where our planet and its precious fauna and flora can find their own balance without our interference, places where species can repopulate, where air can re-oxygenate. But more than that, we need it for ourselves.

The wild calls to us, it feeds a need deep inside us for something beyond what we have created, something bigger than us, something untamed that can pry loose the knots in our psyche and blow away the dust. Most of us don't live near places of uninterrupted wild. We have to make do with the pockets that patchwork our domain. And they are there if we look, if we notice. They are where the birds sing.

The ultimate in experiencing the wild in life is God. In the developed world God too has been cut out or tamed to fit in. But just like wind-blown seeds, the Spirit has ways of finding our cracks and crevasses and making them green.

The pieces in this book are my response to the wild places in my life – in the countryside, the weather, my garden, my God. I trust they will help you to discover your own.

Spring

Equinox

This is it, the official beginning of spring. Oh, the long-awaited date and season and sun! The sun is white, sitting over the tops of the houses to the east, diffused through the thin cloud that heralds the start of a glorious day. It is still cold from early evening to early morning marking the hours of the sun's absence, but it builds to a level of warmth you can live in during the day.

I love this day, the changeover from winter to the early train of summer. I love that everywhere today is the same; we all have twelve hours of day and night – equal night, equinox. And as we sail smoothly into our opening light and new season of warmth, so the south tilts into its fall, into darkness and the call of winter. Today is a magic day, yet most people won't notice it save perhaps a smile at the newfound warmth of the sun. We live on our planet like strangers, not recognising its journeys or its moods, sheltered from the weather and with a ready light to hide the dark.

Celebrating an equinox or solstice is not the prerogative of pagans, for how rude not to acknowledge the birthdays of our home, not to enjoy the relationship we have with the earth on which we live all our days. It enhances – not supplants – our worship of God, for the ground of all worship is wonder and awareness. All creation declares the glory of God, the new sun rising, the hazy air sharpening, the primroses covering the lawn in gentle yellow welcome, the quickening of spring awakening the buds, releasing the call to life that echoes in our blood.

I desire to be out here today but I cannot, so can I take these elements of earth and air and fire and hold them in a burning cauldron safe in my heart? Can I ever trust as trees do, or will I always bother and fuss before I find the narrow path? Is that part of the human condition, part of my makeup; a jigsaw dance between the bother and the bliss; learning to carry all the bits equally well, living in memory and faith at the same time; trusting, trusting as trees dig roots into deep soil, trying to enjoy all parts of the journey and not just the destination? Today I have things to do that will call me away. Today I hang my needs on the wheel of the sun and let it turn me.

Awake!

Awake, awake, blow wide the curtains of the mind and scoop up scattered thoughts!

Awake, awake, beat furrows in the murkiness and mud and prepare the seed for harvest!

Awake from our houses and fences and safety; awake from our darkness and sleeping and winter; awake now for spring is here! It is bursting through the air from dark clouds; it is budding from the soil in new paint; it is shouting from the trees in green song; it is cutting back the night in fresh dawns.

Awake, awake, there is music if we listen! There's a fanfare in the hail; there's a drumbeat in the rain; there's a trumpet in the wind; there's a bugle in the sun. Spring is come. The ragged grass and moss are cut; the mud mounds cast by worms are squashed; the branches on the ground are cleared; and we are getting ready. We can smell it in the air; we can feel it on our skin; we can hear it in our feet; spring has come and we are ready!

On the Cusp

A new start for spring. That means for awakening and unfolding and new colours and shapes and thoughts and sunlight shining and rain clouds storming and animals coming alive with passion and foolishness in all their mating rituals.

It is the beginning now, the second day of spring, so we are on the cusp. The nights bring frost and the days bring warm sunshine. We are like deserts, like mountains. The crocuses have gone, and primroses, violets and celandines take their place while the bluebells prepare for their turn. It is quite glorious. The lawn is newly mowed and is a carpet of bouncy green to walk upon. It invites your feet and your heart into its open space. The trees are still bare, but the buds are beginning to show. A bird is singing.

This is the time to take internal skis or surf boards and launch off on the swells that are all around. It is time for trimming, tying and mending so our feet and our heart are ready. New dreams are waiting to be born, new friends to be found, new pathways explored, new ways of living lived out. It is time to open the cupboards and bring out the good and sweep out the stale and the old. And it is a communal dance, gathering together under friendly skies, working together in the gathering days.

The Birth of New

This old world can feel the same, day by day, but hidden in pockets is the miracle of newness. There are new flowers in my lawn. Some are where they were last year and share roots of sameness; some have flung themselves further, an adventure of yellow pattern on green lawn. There are leaves everywhere that burst out of brown bark like naked puppies, new for a new day, tasting the air like whales. There are broken bits of branch blown down by the wind, stones heaved by winter soils, forests of seedlings colonizing my path, all exploring chance and change. And each time I look it is different, a different view and a different thought, tumbling together like water and ice, making moments, framing memories.

Where do new thoughts come from? Are their seeds a part of the fabric of soul or tissues on the wind? How can our world contain so many without blowing like a balloon? Where do the inner worlds live that contain them? Do I have my own or do I share yours? Does the energy of newness crinkle around them like heat waves from baked bread? Does it butt and buffer and tease and swell and make ripples and folds in space until matter cries out to be reborn as it is squeezed in new directions? How do we take newness so for granted? Should we not celebrate its arrival like the visit of a queen, royalty touching common ground with each flash of inspiration? Where are the fireworks? And how can I shape my head to notice better and to tend its own creations?

The Thing about Spring

The thing about spring is it keeps you on your toes. It shakes you awake each morning with a bracing chill unlike the languid heat of summer or the cosy hearth-warmth of winter. The sky is blue and promising sun; the air is quickening and moving and ready; the leaves are growing and the fern fronds are pushing and uncurling; the birds are all a twitter; and the air is bracing. Through the day you can walk through warm pools of indulgence chased by cool winds of purpose. The clouds play the same game, chasing patterns of change across the sky. It is cold; it is hot; it is sharply, freshly wet; it is suddenly dry; it is teasing and moving and exploring and growing and full of the energy of life. Here comes a shower when I started in sunshine, and who can predict the changes that will cavort today?

There's always more to do in spring: tending newly-grown gardens and removing dead wood and leaves and daffodil heads, spring cleaning houses and thoughts and ways of being, and erupting onto the new stage that spring brings. Change is unharnessing the old, trying on the new and finding as we do so that we are young again. Although the sun and clouds play chase and you can never tell which one you will find in the sky, the sun is winning as the days grow in warmth and light and abundance. And we are dancing; we are shedding winter coats of heart and treading greyness of thought into an early grave. We are whipped by the wind like the leaves on the birch tree until we find ourselves bare and ready to move or linger, dancing with the pulse of this time.

Violets

The sun shines; I come. I sit in the gentle air, in the waiting warmth, in the bowl of blue and am welcomed into spring. Spring – and holiday. It is still and timeless like memories of summer. The birdsong is all encompassing; no longer in the background, it fills centre stage with murmuring, cooing, and sharp, sweet trilling. The trees are opening their arms to the sun, and you can sense the surge in them as buds are fed ready to burst with green. They are swelling from the grey bark like remembered dreams – ready but not rushing.

It is the daffodils that cheer the heart, even when the sun is slow to show. How wonderful that the first colours of spring are the colours of sun, so bright against the lawn, just-mown for the season. Daffodils, celandines and primroses, and yellow mahonia blossom just opening to release its scent.

But there is more. Scattered through my garden are wild violets, dark purple – hiding from first sight – and white and mauve too, the only flower in the rainbow. There is something thrilling about noticing the presence of something I haven't planted, like a gift, like angels visiting unawares. We take it for granted that weeds blow in, but here is a bounty of beauty I didn't expect.

Is God like this, scattering violets in our path to cheer our way, even when we don't notice or return the thanks? It's so easy to notice the weeds along our way, and they will always be there. But scattered between in cushions of colour are violets – God's gift.

Gloom-mood

So here we go, gloom-mood... Let's have a poke at you; let's have a rattle of bars, a shaking out of sheets, a dripping of lemon juice into the oil, of sunshine into the murk. Let's invite you to ride a train – where do you want to go? Let's imagine things you like – what do you want to see? Let's think about believing and trusting and enabling and dealing gently with limping feelings. Let's think about the good feelings we often get and smile as we remember. And let's pretend we're cool and walk out hand-in-hand to peek at the little patch of awesome world nearby.

It is grey and blowy. What can we imagine? I can imagine the air whipping through the trees with a smile on its face and golden hair and a long orange dress. I can imagine the air as a gift that has come, gliding and riding and bumping and climbing, all the way from America, sweeping over the heavy, heaving ocean. I can imagine the air as a huge body of breath that fills my lungs with a scent of the breath of a million others. I can imagine the air listening, holding the echo of our voices, absorbing the range and pitch and throb and beauty of our music. The air is like my writing. I cannot see it but it fills the spaces between me and all things, and although it sometimes surges or strokes or scents, it is just as real and just as present when it is still.

Hidden Stars

The evening is cool, close, dark. It feels like this world is the only reality. I cannot see the stars, I cannot see the clouds that hide them, but it is night and I know they are there. They are hidden now but even more so during the day when we live in our blue or grey world and imagine them part of the night. Bright berries in the sky hidden by light as well as by obscuring cloud, never to be seen at day but still there.

Other things are hidden: our dark parts, like clouds in the night sky; but also our inner beauty, like forgotten stars. Although I don't like dark things – don't like accepting my failings – often it is inner beauty that is more difficult to accept. It is never seen – like stars at day or covered and filtered by scudding clouds – yet it is my deepest and most real being. How might my life be if I held on to that beauty and believed it of myself, if I looked for it in others?

Good Friday

Oh, what a thing that Jesus should die for me, for us, for all who were slate-grey stone towards him, to die for hardness, for sticky selfishness, for hate and desire and fear and all the cocktail of emotions we use to abuse the paths of peace. How could he make such a dirty thing come clean; what is this strength of love that can hold evil and death and be transformed, not tarnished? How did he feel when he held each of our wobbling hearts and knew their pain and their recipes for disaster? How could he love so much that there was no crack, no room for revenge? How could he be about such a big business as saving the world and still be there for his friends, for us? Is this how it starts? The small local loves that don't crowd the heart but furnish it with care for the more? Is that why we can feel it now not as an equation of justice but as a tender trusting of love?

How long will it take to know the depths of this love? After I've fashioned a new heart for myself, a new path to pursue, there's still more, always more, encroaching on staleness, unsettling any resting place that has become too cosy a home – for it is not finished; there is always more. Love doesn't stop and stagnate; it moves and laughs and lives and calls and heals in ever bigger circles as we set our inner compass to follow its way.

Easter Saturday

Easter Saturday and all is quiet, the clouds holding the sky like a muffler. The colours of the flowers are dimmed, there is a snail sitting on a leaf of the wallflower and gulls fill the interstices of the silence with their warnings. It is the waiting day, the day when the broken egg of dreams has seeped away and all hope seems hidden. It is a day when the grief and questions of yesterday cannot run their measure but sit tight on the chest like a box. For it is Sabbath, it is God's day, and he has the key which he will turn at first light tomorrow.

What do we do with waiting days when we cannot rush to the scene of our sorrow? Do we pummel the air with words or wrap the blanket of emotion around us like a skin? Can we attend to anything, or are we trapped in a time-warp like a tunnel, waiting to touch the source of our pain, to bathe the body of death with our perfume? Can we feel the God who holds us, sharing our tears, offering the cauterising of peace if we would accept it?

When our interior world is in meltdown we don't easily see the external; we walk in our wound, not in the world. But there is a hospital for the heart that can help hold our pain, the scent of the wallflowers like a salve, the yellow carpet of primroses like a basket for the heart, the fresh green growth a promise of life and strength and new tomorrows, a prescription for hope. The birds keep watch for us, and we can wait held in the web that is our life here and that strings our heart to heaven.

The Day of Easter

God of the glowing and the knowing and the growing, break forth within me as I breast this day. Break forth from all the stony wastelands, the dead dreams, the ancient aches, for this is the day of Easter and the breaking of the grave. This is the day of your body burning anew in the quick pulse of life that is now synchronised with eternity, a beat that is burnt into the rhythm of the world, into tortured hopes and wasted years, into my heart and all filled with yearning. This is the day when the wave crests quietly, ready to roll and flood and fill and burst dangerously, wiping out the old with its deluge of delight, with the surging and excitement of a force that cannot be tamed or held hostage but that breaks forth in the power of life.

We get it all wrong, think that the strength of stone and the force of punishments, threat and revenge are the victors, the necessary armouring to protect our fragile beings. But near the path there is a tiny shoot emerging, green leaves I could crush in my hand that have eased their way through stone. And that other stone that was rolled away in another garden wasn't the triumph of punishment and fear but their breaking, the energy of love, the example and offering of a new beginning.

Easter Thoughts

Easter Sunday. Happy rising, Jesus! Happy rising, world! Happy new life and source of hope and promise of overcoming darkness! It is snowing this morning – real snow, unlike yesterday when we had storms of sleet that erupted from the air in waves then vanished to be melted by a tepid sun, only to burst in on us again. But nothing laid. This morning we had big feathery flakes like little clouds bringing their own silence with them and then settling in patches of white. The kids are still asleep and have missed it. They'll just see the remnants on the roofs and lawns and not have their hearts enlarged by the majesty of the falling.

Easter Sunday. They say that fifty seven percent of people in this country believe in Jesus' resurrection. It is part of the story that over half of us live our lives upon, that lines our soul with wonder should we care to look. And we are so used to the story – used to celebrating an event that happened two thousand years ago yet echoes still today – that we can limit its ripples. Surely if Jesus' death and rising so long ago and so far away can touch me now, then one of the things it means is that my life too has ripples. Things I dare to do spread beyond my page and colour others' lives. We all contribute to this pool of life, good and bad; we make choices for righteousness that often sting and stretch us beyond who and where we want to be, invisibly alter our planet and build a platform of possibility for others to stand upon.

Another message from this Easter day is that the dog-eared acts of dirt or hurt that we or others sow can become the soil on which we build our triumph. The universe is weighted towards good; the light will consume the darkness; we can rise above our mistakes and vanities and troubles, and the marks they leave on our hands and feet and in our side will be signs of glory not defeat. We are children of clay who can rise and drink the draughts of heaven.

Carrying Worlds

Oh, to be alive, to be sheltered in a world of such intense variety and measure, to be able to see and know the sights around me, and judge and carry their import on my way. To sit here in early-bursting morning with the light newly bouncing from horizon to horizon, the sky a half-awake mist that will be teased back to reveal its promised colour, to see the yellow of primrose and cowslip surprised by blue as forget-me-not and bluebells and violets and vinka take up their place with grandeur. The air never sleeps; it carries the scent of so many flowers and the touch of silk on skin as it holds the space that surrounds us. I pour it all into my body, an inner bath that doesn't grow cold but seeps into my blood, my toes, my skin. I carry worlds as I move, and I can bring to this world my treasures and my pains, holding them in a basket of thought as a prayer.

Today I will collect more; I will rub against strangers and friends and traffic and noise and world events and we will inform each other. Today these brightly coloured memories will form part of my path, each laying themselves down to be trodden into soil as I pass, a fertile store of organic goodness that becomes a bed for seeds to grow, thrusting their thirsty roots into this morning's sense-feast and sucking up smiles for food that will change the shape of tomorrow.

Chaos and Order

I am on the boat gliding down the canal, looking at the trees and the patterns they make with the sky. I am ignoring the industrial wastes that we pass. In the beginning, was it all like this? However little there was, did it have a light and a dark side? Have there always been things we would consider beautiful or ugly, useful or useless, safe or dangerous, ordered or chaotic? And are the things that we think dark as integral a part of life as the light? Can we have light without dark, order without disorder? Does one feed the other, hold the other, enable the other, take the waste from the other? Can we say one is good and one is bad?

So when I seek God, do I favour sunlit leaves? Do I always ignore the untidy edges? Or can I find God in the mud, in the chewed leaves or broken branches, in the litter or the dogdirt, in the brambles and the flies? Can I see God in the bricks of a building, in factories and lorries, in rust and rubble and graffiti and knives? Can I see God in the people that I pass? Can I see God in the shadows of my life?

Returning home means facing chaos and loss, the result of gatecrashers at my daughter's party. My home is like the world, with intrusions I can't control and don't like or want. But this is it. I mourn the mess and brokenness and random destruction. It is my world and I cannot shut it out; I can just trust God to give me shelter. Being part of the world's chaos is part of being alive.

Love Can Handle Them

I'm in my garden in the spring sun, warm in the cool air like Irish coffee. There are bees humming in the mahonia flowers that spill their perfume in eruptions of yellow. Some tulips are tasting the cool air like morning tea, proper and erect; others have no discretion and have peeled back their petals to reveal all.

The pear blossom is out now, white shining on dark wood, and the wild patch underneath has a carpet of yellow – primroses and cowslips, and a few false oxlips that are a mix of both. Interspersed in the yellow is the deep blue of grape hyacinths and the pale blue of forget-me-knots, the pinks and purples of a few primulas that have seeded themselves there and the violet of violets.

I am back home refreshed from my holiday – a week's Sabbath of no work or complicated planning, just resting and reading and walking and loving. Where better than Dorset? Love needs its roots refreshed and time together to let the other roll in with quiet waves instead of bouncing off the sea walls our busy lives erect. Time to enjoy each other's closeness and to notice that the little games I play that don't best serve love. Love requires us to know ourselves and to accept the way we are with compassion and humour. But it also gives us the fuel to change, to bring love like a needle unpicking a knot, like a lotion smoothing out a tangle. I don't have to be afraid of my inner demons and weaknesses; love can handle them.

Inner Worlds

The apple blossom is out and gorgeous. Each bud is dark pink when shut, pale pink when opening and almost white when wide open inside. The grass underneath has petal confetti dropping onto it in the slight movement of air. I am here without a coat, thinking of the adventures we will have today. The petals still drop, and will do whether I watch or not, whether I notice or just sit here in my own thoughts. What a miracle that is, that I can inhabit two worlds at the same time – the inner and the outer – each one lapping at each other like the ocean's edge, slurping and sucking and breaking and boiling, mixing spirit and thought and colour and shape, taking it in, rolling it about, rounding the edges, playing and spraying it into new patterns. The bluebells' blue haze now decorates part of my marrow; the breeze plays ripples on my spleen; and the apple blossoms, they dive straight into my heart.

My Jenny-dog lives there all the time, walks through my fields of heart carelessly and flops down in her warm corner with little legs next to her nose and fluffy ears falling about her face. Then she sighs with contentment. I guess she will remain there even when she is gone from here; my world is populated with memories. And I can change them and use them; I can hug my Dad who I didn't hug enough when he was alive; I can talk to him and put things right. I can find the dark corners that scare me and bring them into the light. And that little girl, the frightened me that likes to yell loudly at little things, the one I used to try to shut out so she yelled louder still, I can welcome and bring into the warmth and fullness of my life now and see her learn to smile.

Waiting

The sun shines the peaks of grass, the blades of it, now lying along the length of it, wavering and wandering as the wind ruffles the lay of it, and blinking on and off as clouds queue up to cross the sky. It is easier to wait in a quaking world, noises and movement riffling in place of thought, the sun salting the minutes, the clouds travelling on even if I am stopped.

I don't find waiting easy. And I don't agree with 'waiting for God', as if God isn't with me in the waiting. Waiting with God is more like it; it could be savouring the moment, noticing the richness around. It could be snuggling into the day like into clean sheets and letting wonders and wisdom sneak in when they're ready. It could be playing with time, enjoying each moment, eating it up to see what taste it brings. It could take a small space – a few minutes, one head and body, one point on earth – and make it into a huge space that can fill and touch anything, everything.

Waiting must be part of the character of God: waiting, holding, allowing, being. Waiting with God can be a seed bed for life. It can fill my pores and anchor my boots and cushion my head and hold me round the edges. It is full not empty. It can be my peace in a quaking world.

Wild Places

The hazel and hawthorn trees dapple the foxglove and campion. The bracken breaks through like a bishop's crook, the brambles arch and the nettles gather. They hold silence like a living quality of air, broken by birdsong and bees' hum and the river stroking stones in the hollow. There is a magic quality to wild places that restores the soul.

So what of ourselves? Do we allow wild places to grow in rampant chaos, or do we cut and control our inner being? Is there room for birdsong in our plans and processes; do bees visit our memories? Do we allow nettles and spiders as part of our harmony, or do we prefer manicured thoughts and concrete paths? Can I breathe in an inner silence; can I trust the pillars of trees that border my feelings? Are there rivers I listen to although I can't see their source or destination? Am I green; can I make my own oxygen?

And when error or disaster have bulldozed pain through my orchards, can I give it time to heal, can I let new growth cover the scars and enjoy the wild flowers that thrive in new-made clearings? Can I trust that the chaos of wild places is as important to my creativity and sanity as my carefully constructed buildings?

Hello May

It is May and the mayflowers shine brightly overhead as the hawthorn roofs the space I sit in. Its baby leaves of yellow-lit green have found their fullness now, maturing in a month to maternal bearers of blossom. The buttercups have joined the wash of wildflowers tangling in the grass, and the blue of the bluebells still lights dim corners. The yellow palette is now brushed with white as cow parsley and hawthorn line country roads like bridal paths, and horse chestnut and lilac lift their blooms on greens and gardens. The white clematis has hung itself in a curtain from my roof so that each time you pass the back door its scent intoxicates you. It is May and the greening of the trees is now completing, waiting for the ash to fill out its feathers, ready for the triumph of summer.

May is my birthday month – and one of my favourites as all the trees are ready and the peony bursts its big, showy buds at the end especially for the occasion. Why is it then that as a child I thought it a boring time for a birthday? Why did fear loom so large? Why didn't I trust the goodness that surrounded me? And how did the spool of life unwrap that darkness and deliver me into the light?

The length of life is a marvel, holding a myriad of moments that can transform the hardest heart, wooed and unsettled by God. There is such generosity in each new day as the night wipes away the foolishness of failure and enables us to begin again with a fresh wind blowing. There is such forgiveness as the earth buries the blight of the past and brings new life from its soil. There is tenderness and toughness as we should require, the blossom brought forth from the wood. And there are people to act as friends of our heart offering insight or nurture or cutting loose.

I Love May

I love May. Everything is here, newborn after winter's absence, fresh green and glowing. The newly hatched leaves are translucent and are as perfect as a baby's toes, eliciting the same surge of awe. The trees swell to their full size, and you can just catch them in their playdays – unfurling fingers, learning the lure of the sun – before they settle into the majesty of their maturity. The world is green again, and for a moment it is surprise, it is joy, it is balm, before we acclimatise ourselves and it becomes backdrop to our everyday occupations. I love the green; I drink it in deep breaths to water my parched heart.

And not just green. The hedgerows are bright with white, hawthorn flowers above, cow parsley below – not the cultured pink of cherry blossom but mile upon mile of the bounty of the wild. They shine as you drive past; they declare the winter dead and gone and celebrate the opening of the earth.

In May the sun can warm you mellow, playing remembered tunes on white skins. It calls you outside, out of the dark domain of buildings and into the open air, newly refurbished and ready for custom. And the air, the air is sweet, perfumed by the abundance of flowers so you don't even need to hold one close to smell it. The scents mingle with the sun to bathe you inside and outside with splendour. At my house there is a waterfall of wisteria blossom over my porch door and a cascade of white clematis over the back so whenever I enter or leave I am filled with the smell of May.

The Way of Lingering

Ooh, magic, magic! The garden is full of soft sunshine and dappled shadows, the scent of blossom, the hum of bees and the song of birds. It is a gentle, beguiling world softened by the play of shadows which still hold a little moisture from their night's sleep. The leaves of the birch tree shimmer in a dance with a quiet rustling as the breeze lifts them, then lets them go. All the leaves are offering their newfound shape and greenness to the face of the sun in a harmony of belonging. The air is warm in the sun like silk, and you can feel it carrying the fullness of this day as particles of pollen and scent brush across your skin. It is a Sunday, our Sabbath of time saved from the routines of busyness so we can linger in the delight of the day.

Have we lost the way of lingering? Can we still notice the small wonders around us and store them in our treasure-box? What difference would it make to our busy lives if we took care to let each beauty amaze us and fill us before going on our way, if we stopped to smell the flowers fronting the gardens that we pass? Do we feel this is our world; do we live in the mutuality of it and enjoy the offerings of bird and flower as gifts given to please us? And do we gift them back with a smile or a touch, knowing our pleasure is a blessing? This is the place to learn to listen, to live without the carapace that often guards us, and to find that the beauty we can see in ant and leaf and bud is the beauty we can find in our soul.

Happy Birthday

It's my birthday today, a celebration of being born, of being clothed in earth-flesh, of being given a place here to make my own, a citizen of time and space, a breather and believer. I have a body of beauty, a brain of complexity and a spirit of eternity. I have feet to walk and eyes to see far and near. I have tongue to taste and skin to feel and ears to hear. I have permission to be here; the world is my home. I can sing and wing; I can play and pray; I can discover and learn and enjoy; I can change. And tomorrow is always a new day.

But today is what's here and breathing for me now. Today is my place of possibility, my guide to all things bigger than me, my way for learning to live with my feet on the earth and my arms in the air. Today has glory in the dust and scent in the waiting, in the being, in the space around things and thoughts and movement and relating. And it is all there for the taking.

Spilled Sweets

It has rained through the night, and now the garden is fresh and wet, full of the scent of it. Any breeze causes another shower to fall as the trees loosen their stored drops. They look as fresh as someone after a shower, exuding clean, wet happiness. The hosta leaves are holding the bigger treasures, round jewels you can see through. The garden is full of sound as birds and insects celebrate, and you can sense the smell of watered soil underpinning all. Some days the garden seems shut behind its own invisible walls or maybe beyond mine. But today it is open and invites you to enjoy its largesse and be watered yourself, along with the plants; you can be part of this community.

The air still holds the scents of blossom, now freshened by the smell of grass. The scattered petals make patterns on the bench like spilled sweets, and I am attended by my dog on my left (hair curling with damp after her garden explorations, a slug on her back and little drops of water on her nose) and my cat on my right (sitting carefully in fluffy dryness). The dandelion heads, though, have lost their fluffiness and are spheres of hair-gelled spikes.

Today is my party day and I, too, have showered and sit here with clean body and wet hair in joyful anticipation. I have watered all the plans and preparations and now wait for the people to flower in random gatherings, dropping their petals like spilled sweets.

The Conversation of Spring

The garden is a magic place this morning, hung with sun-spun scents and sounds, blossom lazily spilling to the ground, birds interpreting the silence. There are bees humming among the flowers and planes humming far overhead, but it is early on a Saturday and not many sounds of people intrude. The space belongs to the garden, and I feel privileged to be allowed in. The green is so new, so fresh and shining. Even the shaded places tingle in anticipation of the day. The oak's leaves are just full-sized, covering its huge stature with yellow-green light while the hawthorn flowers shine white below, enjoying the attentions of the sun and the orange-bottomed bees.

Against the blue sky are red cones of the fir tree, shining like Christmas candles, and green feathers of ash. The apples trees are a more intimate experience: near enough to touch, the branches multi-coloured with mustard yellow and grey-green lichen. There are sprays of apron leaves with pale-pink flowers, a grandmother with babies on her lap. The plum blossom has finished, and in its place are stalks with little green heads ringed with bent stems of brown stamens like crazy hair. They are so tiny now but will quietly swell and fill and colour to become a feast for wasps and for us.

There is a wild meadow underneath. It has lost its spread of colour as the primroses have gone but in their place there are buttercups reaching tall to try and find the sun. Nearer the house the ornamental tree has blossom the colour of blackcurrant milk, fading now as the clematis that climbs through it bursts open its white cups. The kerea is fading too, yellow-orange balls of fluff filling the whole hedge.

There is so much more colour and change in spring than any other time of the year, all with their sequence of opening and fading so as one finishes another one starts like words in a sentence - the conversation of spring.

Summer

Where the Birds Sing

Summer Has Come in Now

The summer has come in now, rolled in with the start of June in sunshine banners of bright and blue and heat and golden air, filling the green fields with sparkling wine and the tight spot in my chest with smiles of arriving.

It is new this year – new leaves, new sun, new promise – but arrives in a coach of memories and anticipation, its pleasure held in the hand of past glories as if to revisit them, as if to turn back time and aging and step again into the pool of our first summer.

The heat heals, seeping down layer by layer through skin and muscle to my core, stretching out wrinkles and lighting up corners until the whole of me feels new and shiny.

The buttercups are singing at the edge of the road, the bees are purring among the bowls of blossom, and I am shining.

Seeds

All around me is green, all grown from seed, a multitude of life and variety packed into little cases. Jesus called the word of God a seed – how subversive! It's easy to think of a seed as a fat juicy bean that we can pick up and plant as if the word of God presents a plump concept to choose or reject. But most seeds aren't fat and obvious.

Seeds are tiny specks of dust on the wind, grains of sand on the soil. They are scattered as widely as the air can reach; there is no spot immune to their patter. They are multiple, a cupful at a time, so for every seed that fails to find a home or that withers with the weather, there is a tiny army waiting to take root. And they don't only root in soil. They bed down in gravel; they slip through cracks in paving; they make their home in old wood. Seeds are wild.

The word of God doesn't loom like a log jam; our lives aren't one small pot for one tender plant. Each time we think or blink, each time we pass the living parables that surround us in kitchen or garden, in factory or office, in high street or mountain, there are showers of invisible seeds cast joyfully windward, a multitude. It is for this purpose: however many are lost to stony eyes or hearts, there are enough that some will break the surface and grow green; there will be fruit.

Summer Solstice

It is the day of the long sun. All evening it has been young, it has been early although the clock ticked its time away and now, as I put my house to bed, there is still enough light to linger in the garden and wonder at the pale sky. When I lived in Scotland it was never black in June, just a hanging grey as I drove home in the middle of the night. It doesn't seem right to ignore it, to tuck myself in to sleep as if any other night, as if there will be night and not a sandwich of day.

I must sit and watch the orange rim fade and the turquoise blue thicken, holding us in an eggshell, holding light behind the dark shape of trees that are as still as a photo. The only movements I can see are planes winking as they pass overhead, drinking in the blue, echoing through it like fish in a silent sea, and an occasional moth blinking its wings at the light. Others are up; I can hear their noises and voices, cars and coughs circling the land.

Is there magic in the nearer sun, pulling our strings like a full tide? Are we beached and birthed by it, drawn into the song that is summer as it laps at the shore of each cell and surges in the streams of our blood? Can we know the heart of it, launched into the blue to follow the sun, or are we marooned in the clay of our body, merely feeling the ripples as they turn and run?

Announced by Roses

Last night was the solstice, but this year I stayed inside, living my life, attending to ordinary matters. I am going to enjoy it as the official beginning of summer not the start of the longer nights, and sure enough the sun has chosen this week to warm us whereas the day before it was cold enough for autumn. Summer is our holiday season (unlike the two week-long holidays in the Bible which were in the spring and autumn). It arrives and I relax into the sun, switch off and unwind, although of course any summer is a mixed bag of weather and happenings. I am going to enjoy it this year and not panic about the shortening days or fear its transitory nature. It is here, announced by roses.

Every road I travel down surprises me with roses. I had never noticed how many there were before. It's as if I can smell them even from the car. I have some here at the bottom of my garden – a muscly, pink, showy rose and a small, white rambler that is simple yet profuse. Both strain towards the sky to avoid the shade.

I have so many flowers that bring interest through spring and so few in summer, but this year will be different. I have planted a summer garden next to the house. It is filled it with plants that will flower all summer, and already the bees visit daily. My favourite is a small poppy that sends up paper flowers of red, orange, yellow or white from the same plant. I am blessed.

What is my internal summer season? Last year it was 'switch off and rest'. This year it is finding my weeds and working out which I can pull and throw away and which have deep roots that I must learn to live with. I am spotting them all and cutting some back so my plant of gratitude has room to flower. Perhaps if I feed the plants they will flourish and keep the weeds in check. Okay gratitude, love, trust, generosity and laughter, here we come!

Baking and Breaking

The crumbs on my table are creamy white, dried in the sun like powdered milk. I cannot see the egg and butter and sugar; they have lost themselves to make cake, sacrificed their shape and taste and texture to make a new blend that can't go back. When I break it I make crumbs; I cannot take the egg out or break off the butter; they are joined and transmuted and changed. They are a new being: cake. But if I eat it my body can break it down again, do a reverse magic to find carbohydrate and fat and sugar, and scoot them to my cells for substance. So then they become me. I am cake. I am flour and egg and butter and sugar. I am wheat and hen and cow and beet. I am soil and rain and grass and sunshine.

So my life comes from their life – the life of wheat and hen and cow and beet. The food I eat has to have known life to give life. So is cake alive? Does life go dormant to spring up again? Is it incipient; does it hover round the edges like butterflies on buddleia, waiting to land? And can cake die? Can it lose the life-present for us as it stales, or does it just move instead into bacteria or mould? And do the chemicals we add to keep it sweet for us protect the life-present or do they edge it out, supplanting not supporting?

And what of my life? Can I pass it on without being eaten or used up? Do my thoughts and words and actions pass on a life-present as well as the gift of my body to the ground when I die? I can birth a child. Can I birth spirit? Can I so embody life that it seeps into my surround? And when given away, does it deplete my store? Or does it generate more like sweet peas when they are picked, like love when it is lavished, like thoughts when they start to form?

July

It is July and the sun is sitting heavy on my shoulders, calling up the moisture from the earth so the air is thick and sticky. In the dappled shade it is delightful if you have nothing much to do but bathe in the heat and turn your face to the occasional ruffle of breeze like a wind-chime in a window. The sun makes all the colours shine like a bride on her wedding day and lights even the shade so there are no secrets. No secrets and no wish to run and tell for languor settles on us all.

The lavatera, the bush mallow, has so many pink-striped flowers it is like a garden fete, loud and overdressed in the corner. The grass, though, is fading, bleaching to brown, awaiting the rain when it will rejuvenate like a magician's trick. There are flowers snuggling near the surface that erupt each time after mowing: white clover and daisies, yellow buttercups and episcopal purple self-heal. They have gone from my wild patch of garden, subsumed by the unmown grass. It requires tending to yield the wild flowers that one wants!

So much to do now it is sun-time and the garden has overgrown itself and the dust inside can no longer hide. So much to do, but my energy and purpose have watered away; I await their return like a flower open and ready for a busy bee but touched instead by a butterfly's dancing tease. Do bees feel the heat? I passed a hebe so full of flowers you could hear the buzz of the bees a pavement away.

Summer is a curious season. All year long I build towards it, lighting fires through the dark of winter and celebrating the advances of spring, but when it arrives it can feel empty. Like bringing up my daughter. Eighteen years of nurture building to the climax of this time, of leaving school and being ready for the big, wide world, but instead of achievement I feel the loss: loss of routine and role, and soon loss of her presence as she starts her own journey.

Skin smells sweet in the sun if you catch it before it coats itself with sweat and starts to run. And I will find the ways of the season as I slow in time with the sun's call.

Flowers

Although I love the velvet decadence and secret sweetness of a rose, and the proud nakedness and curve and tongue of the iris, two of my favourite flowers are the tiny white clusters of privet and laurel. They sweeten the air with no big show, just a smile of white on green where allowed, where not pruned away into tidy hedges. Yet they carry no offense, just get on with their job of being white and sweet, of welcoming bees, of scenting the air, even if unnoticed or unwanted.

So does the clover, waving its balls of white or purple into the air, and so do the delicate daisies and the wild buttercups. All will be gone with the next mowing of grass, but there is no fuss, no regret.

Could we live more like this, getting on with the beauty and purpose of each day? Do the memories and longings that we carry with us like schoolbags, like pollen-heavy legs, add weight to the day so that it loses its sweetness? There is an amazing trust in the flowers of grass or hedge, a living in the circumstance of each moment and blossoming there, just for the sake of it, for the joy of it, for finding fullness in the day as given, whether it leads to seeds that scatter life on the wind or being cut down so another might grow in their place.

The Obligations of the Day

The sun is singing, singing over my head and over the clenched heads of morning-drenched daisies and the few glistening drops of rain that still huddle in the grass. The week has been windy and cool, and I have shut down from the summer and retreated into internal affairs. But today as I walk distractedly down the garden the sun is calling, calling over my head and welcoming me back into favour.

I am carrying the obligations of the day, folded in on them like a fist which is now opening and dropping, opening and dropping like a petal. I have things to do, but I have lost my rush and bother and the hours ahead have stopped moving so fast, have stopped clamping the edge and sucking time into a tight box. There are roses here to notice, sprays of yellow-flushed white adorning the hawthorn, and the lavatera is opening, pink-veined cups with sceptres at their centre.

I will take my troubles and lay them down; I will breathe in and hold the peace of the day, then pour out my pressures into the patient air. I will plant roses in my belly to perfume and still my dark, moving centre. I will listen to the babble of voices there like a friendly aunt, listen and hold their fretting until they feel safe to stop. And I will invite the steady sweep of the spirit of God that is singing, singing over my head to fill and enfold my inside and outside world.

In Accord with its Name

The summer is sizzling the lawn. The short grass has bled its green into the dry earth and has taken on its colour, brown with yellow highlights in its hair from the steady sun. The longer blades are still green so the lawn is mottled with tufts of grass and suckers of trees and with the green of wildflowers that have now come into their own. Clover predominates, trefoil leaves like lace and white flower heads with russet at the roots. In one corner I have a patch of bright yellow flowers waving in the breeze with deep purple below among the clover. The purple I know; it is self-heal – such a powerful name for so unprepossessing a plant. Perhaps previously we would all have known its uses, all have welcomed it as an easy remedy for infections or inflammations and picked it for our wounds and sores. That knowledge is no longer part of the common fund but is kept in herbalists' purses. For us it is just a wildflower but one I treat with respect because of its heritage.

And above, the yellow. How many dandelion-type yellow flowers there are, all glorious in their wild brightness. There are hawkbits and hawksbeards and hawkweeds, not to mention catsears, sow-thistles, nippleworts and various lettuces. I think mine is the lesser hawkbit. I have had them here for years and have never bothered finding their name before. Names make things more intimate; we have been introduced; we have a relationship. I have also found out the name of the wildflower that colonises all my beds, one I always addressed as 'number 4' as it was my fourth worst weed. It is herb bennet, and now I find I have to treat it more kindly in accordance with its name.

God knows our names. We are not random people shining bright or transgressing borders. We are known; we have been introduced; we are ready for relationship.

Clothing the Sun

The sun has hidden away behind the swelling clouds that have covered the sky like a new landmass. The air has lost its bright shine, and rain has returned to dampen our gardens and our spirits. The light is dull and life feels dull, as I had got used to soaking in the sunshine and enjoying each flower and leaf and tree as it blazed against the blue. But it will be back. The grass will make use of this change to rekindle its yellow fibres with green. And the flowers and I will wait.

The thing I love about England is its green; waving avenues of bushes and trees lining the roads, and carpets of grass stretching their green mantle across fields and river banks, gardens and verges. Green is so soothing; it's the colour of peace and life lining our souls. It shows up to perfection on our sunny summer days – our strawberries and cream days when we forget our isolations and live outside in community with each other. But if every day was sun-butter bright the green would be dried to yellow and we would lose our oases of cool.

So I will put off my sandals and put on my socks and shoes. I will mirror the clouds clothing the sun and wear my warmer clothes. I will retreat inside my house, inside my self, and learn the tempo of this day. I will find the jobs to do that sunshine gives me an excuse to neglect. And I might or might not do them.

The Seasons of my Heart

Drip, drip. The rain has stopped, and the leaves play in an orchestra of their own sound, dropping raindrops onto each other and onto the ground, like plastic unfurling, like pebbles walking. The rain has teased the scent of mint into the air and shone up the ivy leaves to a sparkle, ready to smile back at the sun when it comes as the clouds wander on and find other meadows for their pleasures.

A tiny spider bungee jumps from the hawthorn branch. He whizzes down a few feet, sways a little curiously, then carefully climbs back up again. His silk glistens as he rides it home, a trail attached to safety.

The rain melts the flowers, dissolving then onto the ground like a pool of pink icing. All this beauty for so short a season, and there are times I feel its loss. I feel that the world is turning and change is coming and if I sit still I won't be ready.

What is the state of the garden in my heart? Have I weeded or watered any suspicion sowed, any feelers of resentment or fear, any roots of insecurity or shoots of inadequacy? Have I tended it with kindness and allowed forgiveness to walk its paths? Do I allow my inner children to play there and hug them when they're hurting? Is it a safe place to sit in sunshine or in shadow? Is the wind of the love of God blowing through its branches? Can I let it change with the seasons of my heart?

To Live a Life

What is it to live a life, to live a life for God? Surely it is not to shut away from life, to live with hemmed-in mind and bound skirts? Life – this life we live, this life that pours from now and here, that shimmers before us in unmade choices, that stretches behind and before in ropes of love and knowing, that has carved out a place for you and me, a place of our own, of home, wherever journeying may carry – this life is gift to be lived, not shunned. This is life to be tasted and savoured, digested not wasted, filling our stomachs and minds and hearts. This is our go at it, our full-blown flying in the face of it, the haste of it, our teasing out the tasks of it, the planting our ways in it, the craze of it, the daffodil dying and mountain blessing days of it. This is the spot where history and earth tides meet for me, to know the now, to voyage on tomorrow, to plant promises and learn lessons of kindness and sharing, to till gratitude into the soil that I work, to notice the small things that make up my life, my day, my moment, and celebrate being here to notice, to care.

If my life is God's gift to be lived each moment then I can live it in all the colours and phases that occupy my time, not just the ones that offer easy delight but the parts that seem dull and ordinary or that challenge and stretch me, in the noise and chaos and bustle as well as the oases of peace and calm. And each time I find myself shirking or berating the lot that falls me that day, I remind myself that it is part of being alive – a gift that I might not have, but do – and so all that is parcelled in the package is opportunity to grin again, to know and grow and smile and hold and shake and change and be again.

And our 'work' for God? Is it heavy-duty or is a large part of it treating the people and the world we meet day by day with love, nurturing strangers with smiles, encouraging the sun and spiders on their way? Is it learning to let go of the things that twist, and trusting the hollows? Is it simply being someone who others can trust and who works at being a friend? It must, after all, be something that we all can do, not just the great ones. And it will be something that, if we do it well, will bring joy.

Words of Wisdom

It is beautiful here, the sun rising to scatter the white glaze over the blue sky before it makes its way to the front of my porch bringing its hot heat. Holidays are wonderful times for relaxing, for family, for thinking.

Often in books or films, someone will say how important they found their mother's or father's words of wisdom. What are mine? When younger I might have wished for success, a big endeavour that would make my mark and prove my name. For a long time I wanted to learn how to love, which started with empowering the poor and listening to the lonely and grew into learning to love and empower and listen to myself. Then I was learning to trust, to pry my tight heart away from control, away from needing tidy boxes, away from fearing fear so I could let God be big and wild and mysterious and surprising.

But now I know what I would say; I have found the core. My purpose here is to learn to live the life I have been given. Love and trust and joy and forgiveness are all tools along the way. But when I go, when I pop my pod, when I am part of the open-eyed wonder of God-presence that at the moment I just glimpse, then the only gift I can take there is myself. I can find it hard to be myself because I want to be different, unlike dog, tree, stone, sky who all live in their own skin so completely, do their own job so thoroughly. So this is my goal, my wisdom: to live in my skin, to not limit or covet but to enjoy the unfolding of my soul and learn the lessons of my life in the doings of each day.

Weymouth Beach

It's August and the day hangs grey and wet; there is spittle in the air; there are clouds near the ground. The sun is not an orb. His light has been diluted and muted and refracted and captured by all the balls of rain so there is a faint luminescence of grey like an oyster's dream. The gulls don't mind; they still sing their silly song and strut along the wet beach.

There are two tides on the beach, two edges of water: the sea that scoops and scallops the lower sand, and the run-off from the pavement that dribbles and drools down the steps and edges. There is No Man's Land in between, pockmarked with yesterday's footfalls, littered with crashed castles washed to ruin. Their people have all left and will be sitting cosy in cafes or edging and waiting in holiday homes. The most beautiful thing is a gull's feather, lying white on clay-coloured sand, small and silent, collecting drops of rain like jewels.

This is how the day begins. And, strangely, it is easier to walk the beach at first rising when it is flat and empty than when it is full of sunbeams and promise and people. For here it is just my day and there is room in it for me to reach out and touch like the foot of a mussel. It is safe to let in for it is simple and unaffected, a backdrop for love, a table for wonder.

Packets of Weather

The summer has packets of weather that it deals out each day, packets of rain and sun, packets of fluffy white or thickening grey cloud, packets of wind. It is like a conductor in an orchestra: now percussion, now strings, now brass. We are the choir, accompanying it all with our umbrellas or sunscreen, our rushing or lingering, our moaning or rejoicing. Even the weather forecasters don't know which packet will arrive when and where, can only predict 'sunshine and showers'. We are at its mercy and must keep our eye on the sky.

How wonderful in the twenty-first century to have something we can't control, where we are not in charge and must learn to notice, to accommodate, to be flexible. Weather affects us all, even if shut up inside it determines the clothes we wear, the heating we add or remove, the lights we use.

Weather can be a reminder of the Spirit filling our world, beyond our prediction or control, offering challenge and nurture, something we can ignore but not avoid. We can complain and put up our barriers or we can enjoy the rich, moving life force that fills each day.

Summer

I can immerse myself in the bowl of summer, feel its edges around me and sink down, down into its unfettered abandon. The sun is loose and free; it soaks through the air, through the ground, through my skin like caramel. The clouds are friends scattering the sky with white or bringing the rain we need to maintain the green and to open up the earth. The days stretch into the night like a house with extra rooms added each summer, rooms to fill with all we want to do in the light and with all the occupations of nature.

Nature fills summer like an Indian wedding: everyone here, everything so full of colour and life. Flowers follow the sun; bees and seeds follow the flowers; and birds follow the seeds. There is so much – a plenitude – so many insects, so many grasses, so many plants with their own colour and form; so many trees sculpting the shapes around us for light and birds to fly through, filling the earth at their feet and the sky at their head, sounding the wind for us when it blows.

We are part of nature and fill each summer with our open bodies. We cannot escape it, cannot avoid responding to its light, its heat, its pollen. We are changed by it; we are part of the great cycle that spirals through the seasons, carrying us all in its loops. This year I am going to live in it fully, greet it each morning and enjoy its embrace. My mind likes hurrying away to the future and holding the summer in my plans, holding its transience and so anticipating its demise. This year I'm not holding the summer; the summer is holding me. I am grounded in the grass; I am blooming like the hawkbit in my lawn with bright heads of yellow florets and fluffy heads of waiting seeds. I am not yesterday or tomorrow; I am here and now; I am turning with the sun; I am happy.

Open

There are times when it seems the whole world lies open like an oyster's shell, its surfaces shining instead of dull, revealing instead of hiding. Each face and leaf and shape and colour is charged like an ocean of spirit, like a thumbprint of God. All are painted with the same brush, the same loveliness, and I can feel the same life rising up in me to meet them. As they open I open, or perhaps the other way around.

They offer so much more than a backdrop to my walking; they are the pattern of my thinking; they are beauty in my soul. They all know each other, and I am part of the knowing; we are strung together like stitches in a garment, like waves finding shore. And the ocean, the secret smile that filters through, is an essence of joy, of completeness, of God. Each of us is an echo of glory; each of us traces the love lines of God.

As we live we create, making portraits of God, for God. We take our little part of the universe and wrap it in words or gesture, in paint or clay, in steel or brick or paper, and unfold God in the picture of our days. God shining through light and shadow, through shape and colour, through leaf and face. The world is open and God is within.

The Nakedness of Summer

The air is warm against my skin. I love the nakedness of summer; I love the air on my skin so I am part of it, walking through nature open and transparent, not encased and armoured in layers of clothes. I love the smell of skin when it's been in the sun; I love feeling the breeze ripple the hairs on my arms. Even the rain feels good like a caress.

Many days are cloudy but they are still warm, they are still summer, and I can still wear strappy tops. I haven't missed the sun; I've just been luxuriating in the summer, in the season of holidays when school and commitments don't mark the days. I hold out my arms and bathe in it or run like a kid playing aeroplanes with the delight of it. It is more difficult when the sun visits and then hides away as everything suddenly seems gloomy compared with its brilliance.

This is a season for reading, for seeing friends, for exploring, for having adventures. I am untied from my usual commitments and ready to run. I have put down my baggage, I have put off my outer clothes, I have bared my arms and my soul and I have immersed myself in summer.

Breathing the Green

I have been surrounded by concrete for too long, trapped in a town with no gardens, no green. I am making my escape through the low stone cottages and out onto the hills nibbled close by rabbits and sheep. I can feel the grass under my feet cushioning the rock, the thin soil. It bounces with me, scraggy and ill-kempt, browning at the edges – but to me it is life. I breathe it in, careless green vistas, but it is not enough. I sit and let the breeze that blows the few tattered stalks that lift above the green blow in me. We are both thin and brown and bare. Breathing, breezing. There are a few small thistles, and everywhere is carpeted with droppings. I lie down carefully and absorb the blue sky. The white delight of cloud like a message overhead fades back into the blue as I gaze. I want the sky to soak my front and the earth to soak my back, but I still feel brick-bound and tight. Breathing, lying, sky-ing.

How can I download more of the field into my fancy, of nature into the parched reaches of soul? Walking the way, noticing, nature-ing. There is an old boundary that crosses the field, a ridge of history that now has no fence, just occasional stunted trees. They are hawthorn, small but tight with leaf, thorn and berry. The trunk is an artist's dream, split into caves and crevasses, turning and twisting in a slow dance.

Nearby there are rabbit warrens, a dozen entrances burrowed into the earth. When I walk the hill I am not just standing on rock and soil; I am standing on a honeycomb of homes. Are they in there, furry in the dark? Do they know I'm here, vibrating their ceiling with my step?

My need for nature is like a thirst, as essential to life as water and sunshine. I have breathed in green. I can go back to buildings.

Images of Green

Journeys take you out of yourself, out of your normal landscape and its often-heard music. Today I saw poppies, bright splashes of red to surprise the green, growing in patches on verges and here and there – oh joy! – in swathes on country fields. Here and there, too, a cluster of white, elderflowers like large lace buttonholes of clotted cream, and swaying wildflowers waving above the grass and bracken. But today's palette is green, seas of it stretching to a moving horizon, grass mown or tufting, trees full and plump with purpose, filling the eye and the heart with rest. It is a summer colour and the green and the sun fill the space so naturally it is hard to imagine winter; we attune to plenty as children attune to presents, setting it as our compass-bearing for the life we long to live.

But we need this. We need the times of feasting and filling our hollow souls with a surfeit of beauty and restful splendour, drinking it deep, lining the dark, cracked crevices with a carpet of colour, storing the sunshine like honey as food for darker days. And each sweet day trips memories of others tumbling in a waterfall of holiday happiness.

I am a squirrel laying down stores for winter, absorbing layers of light and images of green until my cup runs over.

The Last Week of Summer

Early morning and it is back to my winter coat as I sit at the bottom of the garden. Everywhere is wet and shiny from last night's rain, but the day is dry until a squirrel runs overhead and dislodges a shower from the branches. The sky looks grey, but there is little cloud, just lack of sun. The brightening edge to my left fills and spills as the sun lifts over the sinking rim of earth and shines on the hawthorn, on my face. The shade frames it like a mirror. It is the last week of summer, and autumn is nibbling round its edges.

The grass is so green, recovered from the drying days of sun and glory that brought in the summer, green and sparkling with the gift of rain, dappled with apples and the first fruits of brown leaves. The apple trees are full this year, weighty with their green globes of goodness. The Bramleys last all winter, and I store them like a squirrel to gift on passing friends. Others I leave littered for birds and insects and slugs to enjoy, and after them the mould. What a wonder mould is, decomposing our waste with never a word of thanks.

Autumn has almost come, and here and there a tree has started putting on its ball gown of red or yellow, ready for the dance. They are beautiful, but I am coaching myself to feed on the green while it is still here and store it in my soul. It has to last all winter.

September Song

The wind is on the go again; the breeze is on the blow. It is shifting time, shifting smells, shifting seasons. Autumn is coming. It's not hurrying; it's making the most of the remnant sun, sneaking in on the back of summer. How strange that the fullness of summer, the crops of fruit and grain and memories, should mature into roundness and ripeness not at the height of summer but at its end, a prize given to another season, the taste of summer long after summer's gone.

The leaves are lazily counting the days 'til they fade and spin falling to the earth, just as the earth spins silently to face its back towards the sun. There was so much preparation for this, so much greening and growing, so much opening and flourishing, so much light and hope and expectation, and now it is falling away, fading with the leaves, closing and completing like the credits running over the last feet of film.

And did we do it? Did we live the life we dreamt of last winter; did we surf the days and tie-dye the shorter nights into new creations; did we capture this year's magic, the flavour and savour of it? Did we mount the beast and run at the open door, arms wide, voice yelling for more? Are we ready yet to finish with the froth and spin, and settle for the subtleties of greying days?

Could we capture the wind and send it back to harvest the unused days, or would they ferment and rot like over-ripe fruit? There is no gainsaying it; the world has turned and we are sliding down the dark side grabbing blackberries and nuts to cheer our way. I will find the new rhythms of conserving and warming and planning, I will welcome the energies of earth and grounding, but at the moment all I can feel is the loss and the turning as summer droops to fall.

Autumn

Where the Birds Sing

All is Well

The wayside plants talk to me as I pass in words of brown and green. "Hallo," they say, "we haven't seen you for a while. Are you okay?" I smile and pass on past huge, happy hazel leaves grinning at the sun and wine-thorned stems of bramble resting from all the pushing and growing and arching with a maternal air and nests of black drupes.

And, oh, the red, round earrings, necklaces, jewelled bodices of hawthorn which is modestly turning to dappled yellow and brown so as not to flaunt its pride in such a rich harvest. Elder leaves catch the sun and the spiders and the shape of the day between each leaf as a present to please us as we pass.

Nettles lean drunkenly with their stiff tassels of beads, humbly healing the land with a shy smile. And the grass is still singing as it loves the sky and reaches for embrace before it lays itself down, swayed by the gentlest kiss of air.

All is waiting. All is round and green and well-fed and happy for the year has been won; the roots are holding; the fruits are hanging ready for new times after dead winters. There are no regrets; there is no sorrow for the time that will crumple and blow away leaves and seeds, no fear of bare branches, no awareness of temporary death, just a resting in life, a simple trusting in growth that is part of next season's bloom. Life goes on. All is well.

Berries

There are berries all around me, red hawthorn over my head, the black of laurel behind, deep purple of elderflower hanging next to me on one side and green tree ivy the other, waiting for a colder season to darken.

It is September and we are on the cusp, summer and autumn mingling in the shortening days. There are roses on the trellis and fungi at my feet. The grass and the gravel are speckled with the first brown leaves, but all around is still green and growing.

I can choose my focus, relishing the still warm sun, the inviting grass, the perfumed flowers. Or I can start to let go, to prepare for the change in my inner and outer season when the world will have spun past that place where we favoured the sun and we start the slow wind down to winter.

September is a Full Month

September is such a full month; it holds summer flowers and autumn berries and winter leaves. Everywhere you look there is a feast waiting to be tasted, a full palette of colour, and change rippling through the trees like the wash left behind by summer's boat. The horse chestnuts are first to succumb to the pull of fall, brown crinkling and crumpling the leaves while the conkers tumble smooth and glossy. But others too have a light carpet of yellow and brown although above the trees look green and growing, just a few yellow leaves that give the game away like the first few grey hairs. If you gather up the leaves when they are brown and dried and smell them, they have a spicy, earthy scent that is so evocative of childhood autumns it triggers memories that clothe me.

Some trees are not so subtle. Most maples have a blush of pink, dusting and diluting their green, but one that I pass each morning is deep sea-green everywhere save for a triangle of pure fire at the top, like a cone of magma held by the cool earth. And round the corner the extravagance of a Virginia creeper demands you stop and opens up your cool, tipping in a shared delight that drips in rich red.

There are berries everywhere: red hawthorn and rowan, pyracantha and holly (though the holly feels wrong like a Christmas card sent too early). There are blackberries and elderberries and blue-blushed sloe. There are downy seeds and spiky seeds and burnt orange sceptres left behind. And there are spiders curtaining bushes and paths and cars with their webs.

Sometimes we need these delights when the mellow of the sun cannot warm the cold mornings and evenings, when the night creeps on, when the wind comes to unsettle and change is in the air. This is part of the pattern, our dance with the dark, our awareness turning from the sky to the soil, to deep things, to earth. But this year I have a parable to remember when I feel bare and cannot see fruit in my life. The trees are not lying dormant through winter. When the sap withdraws from the leaves it takes all its goodness to the roots, secretly strengthening them ready for new growth in the spring.

Echoes in the Air

The swings stand still in the garden. The bare patches scuffed by eager feet beneath have time to grow to grass. The waterfall that has been broken all summer will now await another year to function and pour in happy dribbles to the sprouting pond. The slugs are happy, sliding in brown and orange streaks through the wet grass.

There is a birthing energy calling me to listen, calling me to write, echoing in the air. It ripples and tickles, sometimes settling, then wrinkling round the edge. It is an animal that sleeps curled up against the world, and then wakes to walk circles as it sniffs the air.

Today the air holds so much change on its flat surface, so much loss in the rain-heavy day, so much possibility in the turning of the world. The raindrop jewels on the dog's coat have turned to damp curls. The apples, green and groaning, wait in vain for a sunny day to harvest. The brown leaves gather on the ground in small groves that will soon become forests. And the day's weight hangs heavy, drawing it towards tomorrow and the absent sun.

And I, I can sit in the full orb of this moment or I can put it in my pocket and move where dreams go. There are so many worlds to live in, and I will learn to surf the waves where they collide. I am not fenced in save by my boxes, and those I can take and change. The day's weight can be ballast for my journey. The season's change can be seasoning for my soul.

Falling Leaves

I am in the sun. My two usual sitting places are shaded now the sun is so low so I have moved a chair and am sitting outside the summer house, its wall warm behind me, the pampas grass and the sun before me, both shining. I will eat them for breakfast.

There is a sleepy wasp on an ivy leaf nearby, stroking his antennae forward over his face like a morning face wash. The ivy is enjoying the sun too, absorbing and reflecting it from its glossy green plates. I must learn to do that – absorb and reflect the sun, the spirit, the beauty, the love.

The leaves on the ground smell wonderful, spicy and warm. Here is one falling. I love seeing falling leaves; they feel like offerings. When released in a cloud they are a choir. I love the yellows and golds and bronzes and reds; I love the trees with some bare and some still green. I love this season, the colour and smell and movement and change, and snuggling up cosy at night.

Today is unbranched, waiting to see what direction it will bud and bear. I am walking into it now, full of me, full of God, full of light. I am going to value this rare, brief gift of being alive.

Gentle Rain

I like the gentle rain when it fills the sky with soft drops that fall slowly to earth and cover leaves and streets with a fresh gloss. I like the smell of soil it teases out, of living and freshness, and the scent of quickened air. I like the welcome it gives as it opens to let you inside its wet world, clinging bit by bit to face and hair and clothes, unveiling secrets, sharing touches. The grey sky that seems so still, so impassive, is sharing itself with me in delicate moisture.

If it is wet I tend to stay inside, or rush out in upholstered array. But if I stand still in it I can learn more of quietness and the steady business of being than cloistered in closed rooms.

It is not used to being friend as it brings no sunray of delight, no accomplished watering of field and garden. It can seem a little thing, just drops of drizzle. But it can be gift, a lifter of colour, an exposure to the breath behind the weather, a cool sensing and awakening, a taste of nature's rhythm.

Give me a Garden

I am tired; every cell is on standby, my mind resting in a nest of cotton wool. Yet how lovely it is to come into the garden and feel its peace, to see the brown leaves glowing on the green grass, to smell their spicy earthiness where they lie in number under the oak tree. What do people do who don't have gardens to sojourn in or neighbouring fields or woods to wander through? The frazzle caused by my busyness seeps away here; I am earthed.

Each day it is different; each day brings new weather or degrees of season, leaves newly grown or turned or shed. I have created a space here to rest and write, a seat hidden away from the house in my gravel garden with a light for the mornings when it is still night. I make a habit of coming first thing with pages to write or earth prayers to read. And it feeds me as much as the following breakfast. Yet I used not to come like this, my garden lay here to be viewed through windows, or weeded and worked in, unless the sun called me out to sit and read. What I missed!

It takes a while to notice the things that give succour to your soul and to weave them into your life's pattern, not as a duty but as a gift. Things on the other side of now, of the immediate world of thought and action, are always there but can be hidden or forgotten. Give me a garden to extend my roots, to cleanse my being, to restore my soul.

Gifts

The leaves are turning. There is such a palette of colours everywhere I walk or drive, sparkling with brilliance, lighting the darkening days. They are the colours of fire, bold yellows and reds, erupting from the green like flowers. It is the new spring, the air quickening with spinning leaves, each tree changing before our eyes in profusions of plenty, then laying itself down in carpets of gold. They have moved from backdrop to centre stage as they glow and grow and effervesce.

In the garden something has happened to the air. It is funnelling sounds round the houses and into its cool space, gathering them in its pocket. And I am writing for my pleasure, deferring my meditation, my sitting, until later. Will it happen? Can I stop the flow of time when it has wound itself up and got under way (unlike now when it is yawning and stretching and preparing to begin)?

It is early autumn. I have on thin trousers but a warm coat. The sky is grey but dry. And the grass is clean, cleared of all the russeted apples that had fallen and blown with mould, concentric rings marking their march. The ladder is still here, tall and silver against the tree like hope, reaching up into tangled places with shiny assuredness. The breeze is stirring – waking and stretching, then turning over for another snooze. It's loving the oak, tumbling its hair about with its fingers in an early morning embrace.

In the patch of sky to the east – over the fence and the small garden trees, framed between neighbours' houses and dark branches – white is splitting the grey into clumps like froth on a pan and sending them my way. The light has come. It grows like a breath. It is a silent encompasser.

I have one apple here, newly fallen after we picked as high as we could go. It is so red – full of sunshine, just a few scars from its fall. The apples we take are whole and good; the ones that fall and offer themselves to us are broken and spoilt. Seems the wrong way round from what we expect of gifts.

Do they know it's Sunday?

Fairest of fair, a blue sky soaring, circling, winging, singing overhead with just a few light touches of white strung out and stretched wide and planes silently leaving their spun trails. The sun is surprising the houses just beyond and tickling their roofs. Soon it must tumble over and find me waiting here in shadow. It is so still when yesterday the wind was so fervent. The trees take it: the remembered rough embrace, the present elegance.

There are birds flying through the blue with purpose, visiting trees, singing to each other. None are eating the berries that hang in bright red brooches on the rowan tree today. Do they know it's Sunday? Can they sense the lessening of noise and rush out on the streets? Does the worship of a thousand churches fill the air with the gold of Holy Spirit to gild their flight and stroke their feathers? Or is it we who are gilded by their song, shining our space, filling our days with the perfume of praise? And the trees, how they worship with arms held high or leaves tossed to earth in surrender! It is their presence of peace we draw hungrily into our lungs as we walk through woods, through fields, through gardens. They are our air; we dance and weave lives in their fullness.

If we live with feet touching ground and heart held high, with peace in our purpose and the beauty of knowing God in our smile, we too can be air for others to live in that fullness.

Roots and Wings

What a wonderful world we live in. Yesterday morning the sun shone warm as toast and the blue sky twinkled and the sea whispered like silk. Then rolling clouds filled the horizon in a grey, fast dance that brought rain in random flurries. When they cleared the stage, the evening settled into a dry waiting which then quickened and brightened with snowfall. Snow in October, snow on a sunny butter day. And today the sun beams lazy gold while the remnant snow stretches after a night's sleep and falls dripping away.

What a thing it is to be part of the natural world, part of its seasons and daily feasts that we cannot change and that bring chance and challenge and beauty in our way. What a gift to lift our head from desks and timetables and pressures, and touch our toe to the stability of earth that holds all its displays and beings in its moving dance of life. We can have roots here; we can grow wings.

There is a gold light winking at me from the ivy which blinks out when I move my head. It is a drop of water on the end of a leaf catching and reflecting the sun. The sweet peas are bowed from the night's crisping but still offer purple flowers in a last bouquet of blossom. They do not object like we would. They do not stamp feet or drop heads to mourn their passing beauty. They live for the cycle of earth and rebirth, and if we listened we could learn peace and trusting in a way the world we create doesn't provide. The grass is littered with fallen apples, bitten and broken, rosy and shining, and they are as content to be there, food for birds and slugs and fungus, as to be neat-stacked in our shops or melted in our pies. I struggle with the approach of winter, but if I listened more to its way of being instead of grieving the fading days I would find the solace of the moment wrapped around me like a glove.

Child of Eternity

I am a child of eternity, the dimension of God, and yet year by year I feel I age, I feel the sand of dreams slipping through my fingers. But it is only my clay that grows old and tired, not the spark, not the wisdom, not the child within. I have untold springs to count, promises of summer that will quicken not fade.

Each year brings another store of berries to sweeten the winters, of nuts to feed the soul on cold days. I am laying down stores of laughter and memories and wisdom, interbedded with frailty and forgiveness, that will last over when my pod has gone.

Yet the urge to hang on, to complete tasks not yet won, is strong. If I could look at that moment before I follow the light into the dark, what would I want to have done? Would the things that tie up my time now be on the list? I cannot take people and places and things with me, but oh, I can take the taste and look and joy of them and the treasures they have sculpted inside my heart. I can take the wonder and the love and the fields of my imagination, blossoming forever in abundant colour. I can take the strokes of strength I have been able to build in my inner being which will then be hidden no longer. And I can gather all my relationships and weave them into that web of light.

Darkening towards Winter

My, it is dim down here, the days darkening towards winter, the sky hugging its grey close, infiltrating the air. The grey is a colour, is a sound – the sound of birds, a robin trilling and further off a crow cawing. It is still; it feels womblike; I feel womblike wrapped in my scarf and coat. New songs from other birds complete the eggshell around. Are the plants awake? Is this light enough to fire their green cells and start to work for the day? They're probably lingering over breakfast.

The spiciness of the leaves that have started to gather at my feet gives the air a warm edge – hawthorn and oak in a tossed salad of browns and yellows and fading greens. Still dry, it has been dry for a few days now. Beyond where I sit, beyond the rose trellis and the swings, the pampas grass is extraordinary. New fronds feather the air, white candyfloss on sticks, an American Indian headdress of fur and feathers. Watch out for the leaves though; they cut as you touch.

Here I am, me and God and the dog, sitting on all my yesterdays, waiting for the new day, holding it huge and empty like a ball, a ball that will get filled so quickly, so easily. Let us make our mark; let us find our place; let us choose the better way. Let us smile; let us enjoy this feast of being alive.

Rebreathing

Here I am, alive in my beloved garden with my book and pen, my heart like a sponge soaked in sherry but ready for more. I am witness to the morning; I have lain by its side as it slumbered and have now come to live in its light. It rolls over me; the darkness is scattered through the garden, gathered in pockets under trees. I can't see the sun but the darkness is diluting, the air is a cool constant. Twilight, neither dark not light, neither night nor day - a borderland.

I have missed my morning writing as succour for the way, missed the awareness of the moment, of this space, of my trees and leaves and patterns, of the enveloping God. This is private time, and the garden and I are one; the morning and I are sisters; God and I are friends.

There is silence in the morning, silence and space to find myself, to find the day. The birds are my blood-beat; the foxes that come to saunter past, my surprise. The air is moving so gently; it is alive; it is breathing itself in and out of the leaves, in and out of insects, in and out of my lungs. It is carrying messages; it is preparing to carry the sun. It is our invisible envelope of wellbeing, of space between us and other that separates and allows us to find our own truth, that joins us to other so we are all one. Right now it is quietly waiting.

The air I can feel on my skin that I am breathing in and out, in and out like bellows, this air that feels like mine, marooned in my garden, has come, hoppity-skip, from faraway places. I can be breathing atoms from Iceland, from the ocean, from America. My dog is next to me; I am rebreathing her breath. I am rebreathing the breath of humanity. I am rebreathing the breath of my far-flung friends.

The light is growing so slowly you can't see it changing, but there it is, lighter than before, so surreptitious, so inexorable. If we could change like this instead of sudden manoeuvres that clash and startle we would convert the world.

Where the Birds Sing

Up at the dawn of the dawning, the yawning of the day. It is a sallying forth to come down here as the mornings sharpen and darken. The heat and light in the house hold me womb-like, and the garden is strange territory. But here I am, in commonality with the trees and leaves, in community. We all sit with sleep in our systems, the warmth or cool of night in our blood, the slowness of it still heavy in our bodies, responding to the call of the day. Come and creep over us, around us, through us. Come and awaken with verb instead of noun; come and light our fires, stoke our boilers, prepare us for living and breathing and choosing.

The birds are awake before me; they sing gently while the leaves switch on. I am in a cage of quiet with birdsong as the bars. I am solid; I am seated. The rain should be coming later; can they feel it? Does it send a message in the air riding before it? Here is a breeze, sneaking in from the west, pouring gently through the oak tree in soft susurrations of sound, then swaying the ash and apple boughs that line its path before it reaches my right cheek with a cool stroke.

I am sitting under the hawthorn bower with its warm carpet at my feet and a train in the distance, my dog at my side. The blend of leaves on the gravel blends with the colour of Jenny, a rich chestnut, an earth colour, warm in the cool morning. Ivy is to my left and right – a blessing of evergreen where little else will grow or a problem that can weigh trees to their death.

Apples have fallen in the night, full and replete, red and round, submitting at last to the love of gravity, lying as offerings to the new season. The rose leaves at the top of the trellis are catching the light, the new day, and holding it on their plate, offering it shining to the rest of us. It is such a big thing yet it weighs light as gloss, glancing off the leaves in an orchestra of silence.

Embracing the Autumn

Hallo birdsong, hallo dark blue of unlit morning, and cool air, and gently dripping leaves. I have lights to shine my way here, sitting under the bare hawthorn with my feet floored by its leaves mingled with oak. It has been so wet, but in between the sky opens and we can journey forth again with ease.

Some gardens still have flowers, but mine has embraced autumn fully and is a garden of leaves, green of laurel and ivy and fern, yellow of birch, and brown carpeting the green grass. Yet brown doesn't do them justice for they shine with orange and amber, darkening to mahogany when wet. The oak doesn't live in my garden; it is right against my fence but its branches and bearing fill a huge corner; it is undoubtedly lord of this domain.

Autumn and spring are moving seasons, changing from or to the fullness of winter or summer. Autumn has as much growth and beauty as spring. Colours change to lemon or amber or ruby, shapes are revealed and winds blow loose leaves into dances in the air. Wind seems more a feature of autumn and spring than the settled months, scurrying the leaves and clouds, hurrying change.

I have been here twenty minutes and the sky has turned from deep blue to shining grey back-lit with muted light – so slowly that I didn't notice it happening, but here I am in the beginning of the day.

Welcoming the Morning

Mid-November Sunday and the crows are cawing overhead; I wonder what has disturbed them. Not the gently floating clouds moving steadily from the west or the pale blue sky beyond. Not the sun just rising in a silver halo, further south than in summer, caught in the valley between two houses looking like a delicious cocktail. So many other birdsongs fill the air – birds making trills or tunes, talking to each other, welcoming the morning.

How do we welcome the morning? Sometimes I walk through it with my head in the future and my heart in the past, not engaging with it at all. Sometimes it sits heavily on my shoulders, carrying the weight of an overfull day or of jobs left undone. But there are many days when I can capture the early morning before the day begins, enjoying its newness fresh from the east, unencumbered by times beyond. The sun may call me out or the clouds and rain wrap me cosy inside. The wind may have such a conversation that it blows all other thought away, or it may lie still, holding the space. And the birds are always present although it can take a few minutes to notice the sweetness of their song, to listen beyond and not within my thinking.

Some religions may have words or actions to welcome the morning. I just find it and sit in it, welcoming its presence.

The Quiet

Another wet morning. I can hear the rain and wind and darkness outside pressing against the windows and walls of the house, and I am safe in a pool of yellow light, safe in the warmth of my study. The dog is damp as she has been outside, but I am staying in for my early morning quiet.

No machines are on yet; there is no hum, no vibration of voices, no noises save the outside storm sheltering the inside quiet. I can hear the silence; I can feel it filling the room with its weight. There is a clock on the desk, but here on the sofa it feels timeless, the jewel of being held here with only the warmth of my dog lying against my leg and the steadiness of breath for company.

I will sit in the quiet with an inner smile; I will let it fill me; I will colour it with welcome. Then I will carry it with me into this new day.

Dust

I am inside today, facing the furniture, noticing the dust. Dust: the thin, clinging stuff that covers our fancies and dreams. We only see it as something to be gone, hiding and dirtying our substance and treasure, quietly measuring their days.

What is the value of dust? I can draw in it with my finger, print my name, leave a smiley face, connect to earth. I can polish it away, put love and work into my ornaments and surfaces that otherwise would be unremembered. I can blow it to haze the air, a breath of spirit to clean my crystals, to create new patterns as it falls back for another time. I can adjust my seeing so I see it with a smile not a frown, a lens to see the world by.

I can own it, for it is mostly the cells of my skin I have finished with, a testament to my growth and being. I can know it for it is of earth and I am of earth. It is a daily deposit of the substance of this universe that reminds me that I am alive, I am here, I am spirit made flesh, I can worship with hands and knees, I can tread time, I can create and choose and move and love and listen. This gift of earth, of physicality, of cause and effect and learning, of beauty and spoiling, of history and remembering, of wanting and having, of complex dynamic relationship with each person and plant and being, is my arena.

The Hush of Fog

All is hushed. The still air has turned to pearl, wrapping the distant roofs and trees in its haze. The fog gives everything an ethereal quality, filling vistas with a fuzziness that looks warm as a cashmere blanket but that pecks at my cheeks with a damp chill. We are living in thin cloud, muffled from urgency, a fairy land of muted light that shines with a pale intensity.

Close up you can't see the fog, but somehow you can see the air, see it filling the garden, holding open the spaces between trees and fence and house with its presence and its stillness. Tiny movements and sounds of birds are magnified, but they don't disturb the calm centre. The leaves have their own magic. They are picked out in white, frosted into place, sculpting the edge of the air.

If I sit still I can be part of the garden, my breath adding white vapour to the cool mist. I can breathe in the fog; I can breathe in the sense of space, the visible air that holds the moment so perfectly. I can be saturated with the quiet. I can be part of the calm; I can be part of the silent shining.

Soaking in Silver

There is such love abroad this morning. We are soaking in silver, silver wisps of cloud, silver moon that has strayed into the day on a pale-blue, ice-blue sky. The frost has charged every surface with moon dust so it sparkles silver back to the sky like a mirror. But the sun that seems silver as it tastes the edge of the day shines a rosy gold everywhere it looks. Late November and there are still so many trees with leaves that catch the glow of the sun and shine it back to us, warming it further with their russets and browns. Even the branches that are bare shine in greys and greens and golds, although out of the sun they look black against the wash of sky.

It is cold out but so beautiful it is a shame to go in. The frost has turned the soggy, boggy lawn of scraggy green and wind-blown browns into a work of art. If I wait here long enough the sun will climb into the gap between the houses and light up the lawn until it melts at its pleasure.

Love is here amongst the cold, tenderly touching the naked, the discarded, the commonplace, and making them beautiful.

The Womb of the Day

The moon is still ruling the sky in the west, a bright white light in the inky blue, and it is only when you look to the east that you can see the blue is fading, a thin strip of pale sky showing below the grey-gathered clouds. Yet you would know it was the hour of dawn before you ever looked east, for walking through the dark garden there is such a clamour of birdsong. What a wonder that they wake and welcome the dawn each day, no matter the hour or the weather.

The garden that at first seems a dark, alien place is warmed by their sound, and the far rumble of cars and trains, and the distant light in a bedroom window. I have been here five minutes and already the sky has changed, the light is diluting the dark and the blue at the edge has been washed away by pale pearl grey. It is changing fast enough to see the difference but slow enough that you can't notice the changing. It is still; there is no obvious movement of light or colour, just a steady increase of glow. The clouds have disappeared, and now there is a hint of yellow at the horizon, smiling at the still-sailing moon behind me.

We often resist change, the noisy destruction of what is known and the clumsy erection of what is to take its place. But each day we live through these subtle changes that our lives revolve around without noticing, a rhythm of body and earth. Each day brings the gift of new held in the arms of the familiar. I am sitting waiting in the womb of the day, and there on the horizon is Tuesday coming to meet me.

Winter

Where the Birds Sing

Waiting

How fitting – the first really cold day on the first of December. There is a frost on the ground and the air is sharp and still; I was even cold in bed. The sky, though, the sky is bright against the black outlines of the trees, bright enough to find my way but not to read words. The birds are singing as ever and I can see the passage of a plane, its white trail the only cloud among the blue-white pale of sky. People busily leaving or arriving at Heathrow, tired with their journeying, while I am resting here. My journeying is an inner kind, looking for meaning and fulfilment in the jobs that fall to me this day. There is a train hoovering the distance. Otherwise all is quiet and still. Three weeks to Christmas. But no, that is not right. It is today. I am not foreshortening time like that. If I take and live each day, Christmas and I will be ready for each other when it comes.

I walked down the garden through the darkness with no light on, just the diffracted light of the town sky to see by. I have a light here for my writing, but I am in a pool of dark sewn with birdsong. Still so still, still waiting – laurel bush, fern, ivy, lavatera leaves all waiting, waiting for the light, for the errant sun, and for his newborn journey to come. I've lost my dog; she stood on my lap and thrust her muzzle in my face with happy snortling sounds, but she doesn't settle down here when it is dark and cold. She'll have gone back to the lit kitchen and the anticipation of breakfast after ensuring there were no fox trails to chase.

It is busy out there; I can hear rushing cars and a siren but they seem in another world. I am in my glade of green, carpeted with leaves, hung with birdsong and now gently stirred by an enquiring breeze. On these dark, cold days I don't feel like coming outside, but once I'm here the magic starts. The presence of nature is so much more restful than the man-made buzz elsewhere. I start the day with my roots fixed, with an inner smile and open ears, and with peace.

Advent

December comes. It creeps in with the slate-grey dawn past the dark branches to settle with a chill. It is the month of zenith, a cauldron for the dark, backdrop for Christmas lights and fancies. It shuffles hungry feet inside and holds sway round the hearth. It is the month of endings and beginnings, of waiting for the rebirth of sun that now holds our remembrance of the birth of the Son. It is held by the universe of fir trees at our border, framed by laurel and holly and ivy. The sunshine-leaves of brown still floor the fields with the treasures of summer, and the trees prepare to welcome winter.

In the dark we can praise God for lights, in the cold for heaters. Being without can mark our appreciation. And being never without the fine-tuning of spirit since God soft-footed an entry into the whirling world we can lose that edge of need, of promise. So this is a perfect season to tend an empty crib in our heart and prepare it for God. He is coming. It is a silent world outside, gently dripping in quiet concentration. But it holds the seed for tomorrow's turning, for next year's burning, for summer's yearning. December has come and we are called to listen and to wait.

Holding On

It is cold and still; the air is damp and chilled. It is dark in the garden, the sky a deep blue backdrop to the black branches. The sun when it rises has found a different spot to bless with its favours, a new edge of earth to slowly stroke then climb from its shoulders.

Winter is different in so many ways. This winter has let in the cold and begged it stay, arctic air finding a new home, frost painting each surface that isn't hung with snow. Yet still there are trees with a full head of leaves beautifying the landscape like bouquets of dried flowers. We are two weeks from the shortest day and the cold has gripped the branches for weeks so what is the signal to let them go? Are they frozen there? Are they held as a blanket against the surprise of cold? Or are they to cheer our hearts with their round russet outlines and waterfalls of copper coins?

Do I hold onto things that are dead and gone, spreading them around me as if still vibrant and creative, buffering me from exposure, from change? Am I willing to seem bare and barren, to trust in the present and the process, not cling to old gold? Can I learn how to strengthen my roots without having the assurance of productivity or purpose? Can I nurture hope for the unseen and the unknown? Do I dare dispense with frayed accomplishments so that I might have room to birth fresh green growth?

The Tide of Dark Nights

Oh, it's wonderful down here in my own little world. If I switch the light off I'm in a cloak of dark velvet, pierced by the porch lights. The moon is leaning towards her crescent, tipping southwards but still so bright in the indigo sky. Hanging over the garden is a faint mist which disappears as you walk into it for the sky is clear and we are open to the breaths of heaven. Only four days until the solstice, until the shortest day and longest night.

The night creeps up on us steadily, day by day, bringing the cold on its back and leaving it here for the short hours of light. It is so still, waiting patiently for the turn of the year when the tide of dark nights will creep inexorably back and the fullness of winter cold will fill every space between bare branch and open sky. We won't notice the turn as it is in Christmas week, and by January when we have time to notice it will be here already, settled and established.

The seasons always start a little earlier than their date, and winter is ushering autumn off the stage and preparing its props. Yesterday it surprised us with a deep-freeze morning and light snow for starters in the afternoon. Then the autumn drizzle took back the evening – and who will win today? There is more snow forecast, and the garden is resigned to whatever may come. It is starting its long sleep.

Symbols of Hope

Yesterday was the solstice, the shortest day of the year. It hid behind the tatters of snow and the fear of more. It hid behind the focus on Christmas and the bustle to be ready. Silently, mysteriously, we have now moved back from the brink and are inexorably heading into the light, although it still feels the same, although the cold still hugs us like a friend.

The beginning of the return of the sun is also the beginning of winter. We are not abandoned to winter; we are climbing back to the light; we are living in the rebirth of hope.

Hope is essential currency when so much of the fullness of living is shut away. We know the sun and summer will return, our hope is a solid substance that pulls us through the night. In the old days nothing was so sure – the return of the sun hung on our shoulders, our activities, our sacrifice, and our symbols of hope were the living greens that never died, the ivy and holly and their supernatural power that protected them from the long death.

We know better now about the ways of the sun and the cycles of plants. But we all still fear and face the long death. That is why Christmas nestles in its cradle of dark – not just to celebrate the gift of light but to remember the gift of God, coming to live with us when the days were bleak, sharing with us the power to outlast death.

A Harbour of Peace

It rained all day yesterday, and now it is soggy, sitting quietly absorbing and feeling the wetness, letting it ooze and lie, and a little get teased out by the shallow sun. The hawthorn tree is adorned with jewels of raindrops again, like semiluscent pearls. It is a Sunday morning, and you can feel the Sabbath peace calming the air. I can hear the slow rumble of a distant plane; I am sitting still while planet and time and planes move under me and beyond me.

If you listen to the damp quietness you can hear it drip; you can feel it filling the air. The remnant oak leaves are plastered darkly to the ground and have taken up residence as constituents of earth. The faithful grass keeps pace with the seasons, holding the rain and the scattered leaves like a sponge. The sky glistens. It is mother of pearl grey shining with light near the white orb of the sheltered sun.

This day is here holding stillness and breath and being, and we can stride through its waters or soak in its stream. It is always here, holding its own presence, filled with the touch of God, for us to anchor our days. It is a good listener and it can take the fret and fuss of the fullness of our lives and exchange it for a harbour of peace.

White Frost Crisping

What a wonder! The world is full of white frost crisping and holding each blade and edge, and the sky is full of blue and a round sun that lingers lovingly on all the surfaces it can find to warm the sparkle back into mist in the air. The grass is in patterns of sharp white and glistening wet according to the sun's travels. And I, I am sitting outside on a cold December day with the warmth of sunbeams befriending my face and my front – a day with a smile, a day to savour, a day to learn the blessings of surprise.

And we are all held by the goodness of God, sparkling with glittering frost or shining with warmed wet or beaming with sun-stroked honour. Whether we are children of the night or day, we can own the honour of being loved, we can feed our marrow with the germ of God's goodness. And whether or not we knew this before, we can bathe in its message and let comfort restore our soul to its rightful dignity.

Christmas

Christmas Day. The church bells are ringing, a plane is still flying overhead and the birds sing and soar as normal. The sky isn't closed and grey today; it is open with delight, brightness shining from the still hidden sun. What a thing it is to think about God becoming man – a folly or impossibility to some and a matter of common knowledge that fails to thrill for others. Let's mix them up. Let's imagine what it means, what it was like.

It means the easy discourse I have with God, the awareness of spirit in my being and my world, wasn't always there. God as distant, other, fearsome Lord would be what was known and worshipped. Let's think of that God becoming human, and not just perfect, authoritative man but small, vulnerable child. Because for God to become human meant sharing in our weakness and vulnerability, not just our strength.

It wasn't like acting, slipping on a persona while you visit earth for a season. It was a real becoming, like awaiting the birth of a precious child in all their newness, but this time the child was you. Did it feel like coming home, filling the shoes where previously you had only shone in the heart? Did you enjoy the ripple of muscle and the tingling of skin? And the knowledge and love that comes hard won? Did you want to scoop us all up to heaven with you? How did you cope with letting us go and trusting our freedom and inner compass to bring us home in the end? I'm glad you had friends, real friends who were men and women you could live and laugh and disagree with. I would hate to think of you being alone or of a God who couldn't make friends. And you were true to them although they frustrated you and let you down.

What a wonder we celebrate today – the birthing and earthing of God.

The Patience of Winter

Sunday. How quiet it is here although there are distant rumbles and sirens. The birds, too, are quiet; I wonder why? It is 9.30; it is light and the clouds are scudding from and not to the east. The sky is a filled layer of cloud, but you can see the movement by the variation in tone and texture. There is brightness in the sky, holding as it does the sun's absent treasure, and here the air is cool and awake, holding the moment, filling the day.

The ferns still feather the air, nodding softly and enjoying the slow stillness of winter. The ivy keeps guard on its advance position, waiting for warmth so it can move forward again. The pebbles, though, the pebbles are more alert than in the summer for this is their season of cold, grey roundness, their home.

What are the trees doing now; where is their awareness? Has it sunk into the roots as we hide in our homes or does it enjoy the nakedness and bare shape of being in winter? Are the branches aware of holding the sky, and whipping it into wind, the buds like sleeping babies going where the parent takes you without wondering why?

The water that holds warmth round our shores to ameliorate our winter chill freezes and thaws in ponds and buckets and puddles, a dance of stiffening and softening. The dog doesn't change. She still sits next to me, thighs touching in a shared morning encounter, her muzzle oscillating gently as she watches over the garden with her nose, ready for any fox that might chance to pass through. But I am different. The seasons sing different songs in my blood, and I am enjoying the patience of winter.

The pigeons have started to coo. We are all waiting, lost in the large moment that is winter, that is Sunday, that is today.

Wonderland

The snow has come. It is thick and bright, clothing the garden, trees and roads in quietness. A gift of white, of pure essence, poured in whirling skies of wet kisses. It transforms everything, makes the world its own, even gathering on thin twigs and coating the sides of trees. Each bush has its own arrangement, its own sculpture. At night it is still light, capturing the glow of street lamps and reflecting them back.

It is a fantastic time to be shut at home, enjoying the splendour and the isolation. Every window is a picture of wonder and delight, reminding us over and over again of the abundance of beauty. The cats stay in as well, all held within a wonderland, a Narnia with no evil queen.

The snow is a frustration to many, spoiling plans to travel, to be busy. But for those who can take it, it is a gift of peace, of quiet contemplation, of beauty, of delight.

Snow

The sun is shining on my face and glinting off the snow. Yes, we have real snow that shines white and bright. It outlines the twigs and branches with highlights and hangs heavy on the leaves. It squeaks as you walk over it, crunching into compact layers that hold your prints. It transforms lawns into cake-tops, thick, sweet and smooth, but thins on paths and melts from hot roofs. It clumps and collects as it is swept from windscreens and walkways, and along the edge of the road it gathers our dirt to itself like a nurse.

Last night the flakes were falling fast, chasing us home to shelter from the wild. Now they have finished their job and we are invited to look and to play. Can anyone go past and not look, not notice the dark way into the wood lit bright with beauty, the branches arching overhead dressed up for the occasion, the fields stretching nearer in the light, and all linked, all made one with this blanket from heaven that muffles our busy sounds, that reflects the sun into our eyes and fills the cold air with the present of peace.

Love Lasts

It is not quite so cold, not as bitter with frost tingeing each particle of air as it has been. The little patches of hidden snow that adorned the garden for days have gone. And yet still, lying carelessly on the lawn, there is one white lump, remnant of a snowball.

How interesting that gathering snow together in hot, mittened hands and squeezing would enable it to last longer on warmer days. Does that work for us? If we are gathered and melded into a group, a community, a unit, do we find strength to outlast bitter days? What if we are melded with God, what then? Can we then walk in places that would have melted our soul; can we endure when dreams or realities shatter and no longer cushion the air?

A snowball is tight ice. It loses its flaky fronds of crystal as each absorbs the other into itself. Like love. Love is tight; love fills the interstices of our awareness and transforms us all into something else, something stronger, yet that is still ourselves. Love allows the occasion to sorrow or rejoice; love hears beyond sound; love matters; love stretches; love is lost only to be found.

And in the still rooms of delight that pave our soul, love is wall and hearth, door and light. Love squeezes our hearts together into new realities. Love lasts.

The Bones of Love

The sun on the bare branches of the oak tree brings out all its colours so that it shines, yellow-green and bright against a blue, blue sky. None of it could be called brown, yet that is what we might call it if asked. It isn't a simple colour, or a simple being. It holds a covering of algae next to its skin, lifting it high so it can find the sun. It supports branches of ivy and a multitude of insects we'd know how to find if we were birds. We call it 'tree' but it is king and servant of a community and looks as alive now as it does in full-leafed summer.

Winter is about finding a different kind of life to the one we miss from the summer, different colours of soul that we do not notice when full-blown and bright. As the trees go bare we add layers of clothes to our bodies, but the dark can lay bare our souls. This is the time of year when deaths and breakdowns can peak, when we are vulnerable to the footsteps beyond our walls. In winter we need to be held by the network of love our lives have woven. Love that warms the winter cold and lights fires to burn the dross we have carried through the year. Love that faces our mistakes without losing its smile. Love that links us to our own strengths when we struggle, to friends when we are alone, to God when we are afraid. Love that fits our size, the smallness we feel in the large space of world. Love that wears the clothes of this bare season, not a sugar covering that dissolves in the dark. Winter is the time to find the bones of love.

Lighting Fires

It is light now when I rise, a pearly haze of pre-dawn glimmer that lets me see shapes without needing a lamp. By the time I come down into the garden the day has broken fully, but no sun to be seen, just a blanket of grey filling the sky and the branches. It is so wet everywhere, puddles and pools on any surface that will hold them and drops lining every branch. Each day that we think spring might start to approach there is another flurry of sleet or snow, another blast of air from the Arctic.

The birds aren't put off by it; the morning is filled with their song. And crocuses are pushing up regardless among the scattered brown leaves in the wet lawn. Was this once the norm? We have got used to milder winters – bees buzzing and blooms appearing at the end of February. If we lived in Canada we would have adjusted to long winters, but here we struggle, longing for the breakthrough of warmth and the rolling back of icy air. It is as if the winter has parked itself in our souls, and we feel as dreary as the grey days.

What is to be done? Let's light fires to drive away the grey. We have a wonderful wood fire newly working this winter that cheers as well as warms. And there are books to be read; people to be loved; long, stripy socks to be worn; indoor projects to be done; all lighting inner fires of joy that will see us through to spring.

Valentine's Day

Valentine's day and all is quiet. The sun warms the tips of the houses and slithers in wet abandon across the frosty lawn. The wintered leaves still stick in brown batches underfoot – some crispy, some soggy, covering the beginning-bare shoots that are poking through and preparing for spring. The cool air holds the sun's smile like ivy on a fortress. The garden is full of shining surfaces as frost crystals, wet leaves and ice mirror the sun. The birds sing gently to hold the silence of the air like a glass bowl and not to fill it.

Every day is different. Every day holds different surprises as sun and air conspire in changing patterns. Every day presents new surfaces for our inner worlds to respond to. Today, sitting in the sun, there is a peace that spreads like melting butter through any processes of thought. There is patience in the frozen pond. There is openness in the bare branches.

To sit here for a while is to lose one's own manner of being and become, for a moment, the morning. It is to lose the distinction between inner and outer, that hard line of thought, like bread without a crust, soaking the day into every fibre.

So today I begin as I mean to other days, the gift having been given and received, the hope heard, the inner paths prepared. This day is the valentine. This day all is well with my soul.

February

How good that the most challenging month is the shortest of the year, to hurry us towards March and the coming of spring and sunshine and Easter and revelations and new growth and life and abundance. Goodbye February! Thank you for cushioning the winter for us, for being the one to welcome crocuses and catkins, to allow new buds to grow subtly and subversively, and to tease more of the light out of the winter sky, drawing the sun back again with your string of promise.

Thank you for Valentines and pancakes and for the hard clay earth waking up from the cold. There is a bee buzzing; you are letting in the workers of summer. The grey skies are like the mother of pearl lining of living shells, hiding secret growth. And the carpet of brown leaves is broken by merry shoots of green weeds and wild things that are always the first to show. Soon we will have bluebells. Soon the sun will choose our side as his preferred companion and the evenings will unfurl into glad day.

But the buzz isn't here yet, the busy explosion of life under a newborn sun-season. February is still a season of peace, like a mother who rises before dawn and prepares the home while the children are still abed.

Return

Here I am in my gravel garden again. I have been staying away from the cold, dark, dank, bare outdoors after catching a chill. February has felt particularly long and grey although the crocuses are out and the daffodils are shooting. But hey, look at the pearly glaze in the eastern sky where wisps of cloud are trailing the sailing sun. Listen to the birds. Breathe the air. See the few drops of yesterday's rain glistening on the hawthorn branches and the fine blades of green grass, unkempt after a winter of straggly growth and no cutting. There are still pockets of brown leaves, wet and darkening. And bare branches. But new life is beginning; greens are showing on the lavatera, on the flowering currant. What a privilege to be down here; whatever stage or state it's in, I can come into my garden and share in that. I can see it in its nakedness, its drabness, as well as its bright summer dress.

I love watching Jenny's nose twitching as she samples the garden smells, not continuously but turning her head one way – smell – then another way – smell. I love the birds, filling the air with song. And how strange that it is several minutes before I notice them, I am so accustomed to their backdrop. What else do I miss through taking for granted, by not noticing?

I love the purple of the crocuses' fat blooms scattered through the green lawn beneath the fruit trees, dark and pale, with a few that are yellow and white. I love my garden, my space to share with the air, with the growing green, with the seasons, with the weather. I love the green moss that covers the stones edging my little gravel area with a spongy soft carpet. I love the laurel and ivy behind me, always green, always there, and the buds on the laurel waiting to shower me with perfume as I sit.

I love the movement in the sky. At first glance it looks the same grey all over, but there are patches of bright white that are sailing in the opposite direction from yesterday. I love the space here, space to explore and be in different parts, in different moods, but held in this safe place. I love the peace. There are no demands, the garden gets on with itself, the leaves and birds and insects have their own timetable, and I can sit here for as long as I want, revelling in the peace.

The Womb of my Garden

I am welcomed back into the womb of my garden as if I had never been away. It is an arbour, a harbour, a safe place. It is where I too can grow slowly through my seasons. I am allowed sunny and gloomy days, I am allowed to be me, to be unique and yet the same, all family under the sun, all held together by the steady shelf of land under our feet and the soaring sky. I can share air with the ivy, the grass, the birds. There is so much of it, fresh and sweet, charging our lungs and our lives.

What a peace there is here – the peace of growing things at rest, not absence or stagnancy; the peace of muted birdsong; the peace of blue sky beyond the glowing edge of cloud; the peace that the sun brings on a late February day, coming closer at last, reminding us of summer; the peace of green as the grass carpets the garden and the dew carpets the grass, all shining in the sun.

The crocuses will open soon as the shade shifts around so they can catch the sun in their full cups. But you won't hear or see them. They will open as slowly as the moon, as surely as the lure of love targets our errant hearts. The sun comes, love comes, on the green and the brown, the new and the old, whether dead or alive, lovely or unlovely. Here is God ready for us all.

Lent

We're into Lent; it's grey and flat but don't be fooled; we're waiting and preparing for the big events, for resurrection Sunday, for resurrection spring. So I'll bide my time and enjoy the milder weather and make sure I notice the buds swelling out from flat, grey bark into round jewels of lemon-green. The crocuses are up, standing as silent sentinels in the grey, waiting for the sun to tease their fancy so they can open and fill their cups. I have cleared the grass around – they were growing through the carpet of brown leaves, piercing them to wear like a skirt. Only the purple ones remain; the squirrels have eaten all the yellow.

It's possible to sit here and be so taken with the damp grey day in front, or the day just gone, or the day ahead, that I don't notice the birds. But once you listen they are louder than the grey, the coloured sounds shafting the air.

Knowing that spring is coming I can prepare for it, make my garden ready, remove the dead twigs and leaves so that when the clock turns further and it bursts in innocent brightness we are ready. It is the same with Lent, knowing that tending my loss and shadow now will prepare me a heart fit for the overthrowing of dark and the bursting forth of bright life that is Easter.

I am ready. I can taste the sun in expectation; I can sense the spirit of Jesus in hope and joy. It is a grey day but don't be fooled – the breakthrough is coming!

Spring will be Good

Spring will be so good this year, breaking open the heavy pall of winter that weighs its grey cold on the landscape, on the soul. It will call awake the greens from their hidden palette and the daffodil flushes of gold that mimic and foreshadow the warm waters of sun. It will shake and awaken the somnolence of roots, of buds, of earth that have been stilled by the chilled blanket of winter. It will call awake the senses, shut up in scarves and hats and houses, and move us all from dormancy to vibrancy, thrilling with the new surge of life.

The crocuses are here already, but this year they are the purple funeral robes of winter not the first flush of spring. The delicate blossom that usually adorns our tree out front in early March is weeks late. There have been sunny days; there are buds beginning to break on the flowering currant; there are daffodil leaves poking tall through the hard soil; there is light filling the later afternoon corners. But I won't be fooled. Spring isn't here yet for there is no change in the air, no shaking out of winter's coat, no quickening of tempo, no intimations of warmth. Winter still sits heavily here like a guest overstaying its welcome. This is not spring. But how wonderful when it finally comes.

Different Times

I am marooned indoors. The machines hum around me, but I can hear silence beyond that, I can feel space opening up to hold me as I rest after a morning of chaos and noise. Two winter jasmine flowers are peeping at me over the window's edge, mirroring the yellow forsythia in the front of the garden. The smoke bush next to it is still bare, a winter tangle of brown branches, so the sun can find the soil beneath it and lure primroses and violets into bloom. I have a photo of them in front of me as my screensaver so I can see them twice. I love this picture; it looks like a treasure you might find on a country walk, and here it is, part of my garden.

Spring finds us all at different times. Some claim it as a promise, holding yellow cups to lightening dawns, warming the cold air. Some ease tight buds out ready for the sun to explode them into green. Some wait until all else is done, filling the gaps in the hedgerow at last like a bride late for her wedding.

I am still waiting, closed in the cool of winter though the equinox is almost here and the sun sometimes sits full and round like a sun-tanned guest. I have been preparing my garden and my heart, cutting out the dead so they are ready for green and growth and life.

The Last Day of Winter

The last day of winter. Yesterday we were still filled with the grey chill of opaque skies, but they cleared last night to leave a morning of white frost sparkling in the sudden sun. All day long it shone, warming the stage where it played but leaving it still so cold in the wings. It is still winter but not for long.

The magpies are getting ready, trimming thin twigs off the birch and carrying them away to build a nest. Blossom is starting to appear: delicate pinks, not the showy, frowsy cherry pinks yet, and feasts of tiny white like baby's breath as the blackthorn comes into its own. All year long it plays its part unnoticed, just a small tree with small leaves in small hedgerows. But March is its moment of glory, splashing the dark branches with glittering white like waves of surf.

Today we had lunch outside. The garden furniture had all been covered for the winter like a stately home out of season. A blackbird has been bathing in the pool of water that collected on the top. It's gone now as we reclaim the patio, a foretaste of spring.

Tomorrow it will be here, the wheel turned again, bringing the familiar and the new like a bride for her wedding. Spring in the air, in the garden, in my blood. What marvels will it hold this year?

Pieces

Also by the Author

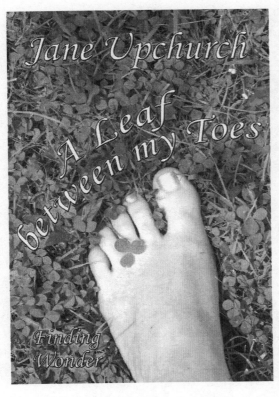

A Leaf Between my Toes

Wonder is a discovery that transforms a dull day.

It enlarges our hearts so that they fill with the qualities we honour. It is a link with what is sacred, a way of worship. If we take time to notice, to listen, to wonder, we are called out of ourselves. It can happen as we drive to work, or sit quietly at home. It can happen on holiday, or as we walk the dog. It can happen in our garden.

Jane Upchurch's insightful pieces flow naturally from a heart of wonder as she observes the natural world around her. From her 'garden sanctuary' she shows that the gifts we take for granted often hold secrets of remarkable wisdom.

Jane's writing links a love of this planet, its rocks and oceans, trees and bees, with awareness of the intimacy and wildness of God. It is a way of growing closer to the things she writes about; it is a way of growing in love.

To be published in spring 2013.

For more information, see publisher's website: www.onwardsandupward.org

Similar Books by the Publisher

My Art of Poetry

Judy Edwards

Art and poetry have been at the heart of Judy Edwards. This is expressed in this book by her love of nature, particularly from her home in the southwest of England. Her paintings and photographs are an essential part of her expression. Similarly her love for her husband, Pete, and her family form a part of her emotional foundation. Over and above all of that, her love for God and appreciation of God's love for her shines through.

A Walk with Wisdom

Luke Jeffery

How can I live life to the full? How can I be sure that my life's purpose will be fulfilled?

Life is full of tough questions. Sometimes we face the questions. Sometimes we avoid them. Often the answers seem to evade us. But truth can be explored and discovered. The key to unlock life's mysteries is 'wisdom' – and it will totally change the way you experience the world around.

This book of wisdom will help you to move forward on your journey, whatever stage you are at, and result in a lifestyle of love.